G000300271

GO FISHING FOR
CHUB &
BARBEL

GO FISHING FOR
CHUB &
BARBEL

GRAEME PULLEN

The Oxford Illustrated Press

© 1990, Graeme Pullen

ISBN 0 946609 91 8

Published by:
The Oxford Illustrated Press Limited, Haynes Publishing Group,
Sparkford, Nr Yeovil, Somerset BA22 7JJ, England.

Haynes Publications Inc, 861 Lawrence Drive, Newbury Park,
California 91320, USA.

Printed in England by:
J. H. Haynes & Co Limited, Sparkford, Nr Yeovil, Somerset.

British Library Cataloguing in Publication Data:
Pullen, Graeme
  Go Fishing for chub and barbel.
  1. Chub & barbel. Angling 2. Barbel. Angling –
  Manuals
  I. Title
  799.1'752

  ISBN 0-946609-91-8

Library of Congress Catalog Card Number:
89-80716

All rights reserved. No part of this book may be reproduced or
transmitted in any form or by any means, electronic or mechanical,
including photocopying, recording or by any information storage
retrieval system, without the permission of the publisher.

All photos from the author's files, 'Fishpix'.

Contents

Introduction   7

Still Water Fishing for Chub   10

River Fishing for Chub   17
    Snaggy Swims
    Open Waters
    Feeding
    Fast Waters
    Touch-Ledgering
    Freelining
    Fly Fishing
    Surface Fishing

Tackle Suggestions   58
    Rods
    Reels
    Lines
    Hooks
    Floats
    Swimfeeders
    Additional Equipment

Baits   69

Barbel   78
    Freelining
    Floatfishing
    Ledgering
    Groundbaiting
    Swimfeeders
    Stret-Pegging
    Trundling

To Bill Pardy, previously the Bailiff
on the Royalty Fishery at Christchurch.

Introduction

To successfully fish a river you almost need to develop a sixth sense of where you think the fish will be and how they will react under different conditions. Rivers are far more affected by rainfall than still waters and the fish's feeding pattern is disturbed accordingly. Depending on local geology, rain falling on land either drains through the surface to form underground aquifers or runs straight off it. As a result, two different types of streams and subsequent rivers, are formed. The first, the chalk stream, is fed by one or several underground aquifers. The rain filters through the chalky substratum to the underground aquifers. It can then bubble up to produce headwaters or springs, the start of some of our greatest rivers. The filtering action cleanses the water of some minor pollutants but also ensures that the water only drains through at a constant rate. Even after a heavy rainfall of several days, a chalk stream or river will only flood gradually. In addition to the controlled rate of filtration, the low-lying patches of land surrounding a river—the water meadows—regulate flooding. They are the first to flood should the river level rise. Situated so close to the normal river level, they are continually wet and act almost like a sponge, soaking up the surplus of water in winter and releasing a constant trickle in the dry days of summer. This type of river is much easier to fish; the usual habitat of the fish is barely disturbed so once determined, the area is likely to prove successful time and again.

In contrast, the second type of river, the spate river, is usually found in areas of rock or clay, both of which are impervious to rainfall. Any rain flash floods straight off the land and into a river. Some spate rivers can flood in as little as two hours and while technically a flood may not be recognised until a portion of the river has burst its bank, as far as the angler is concerned, a flood is anything that upsets the fish's habitat sufficiently to make location difficult.

Pollution of our rivers is a major problem and a toxic discharge can wipe out fish stocks entirely. We fishermen should be particularly aware of these dangers and should anything look suspicious—such as dead fish floating in the river—the local water authority should be contacted immediately, as well as the ACA and the relevant club or day-ticket office. In this way, we may be able to do something to save

Go Fishing for Chub and Barbel

our beautiful rivers from decaying completely—and still preserve our sport.

Rivers and still waters boast many species of fish but with moving water you need a greater degree of tackle control, particularly when floatfishing. Two of the most popular river species that run to a large size are the chub and barbel. I could have written a whole book on each species but some of the techniques for catching both of them are so similar that you are likely to take either species with the same approach.

It is worth noting that both chub and barbel have been caught after being stocked in still waters. The barbel doesn't thrive well but the chub does and I see no reason why the new British record for chub should not come from a still water. Indeed I have fished several that have held fish of up to 7 lb, and sooner or later somebody will take a double-figure chub that has fed on a high protein diet in a trout stewpond. With their appetite, I would imagine that chub would respond well to being hand fed the same way as trout. Both chub and

Profile of a chub. With its quizzical eye, nervous disposition and tendency to live near snags, the chub makes a worthy adversary.

Introduction

barbel can be taken right through the season, from the hot low-water days of summer through to the autumn and into the frost-fringed months of winter. Winter fishing for both species remains a sport for the really dedicated and the chub offers the best chance of success on the cold, raw days of December and January. The barbel will feed of course but only for very short periods when the water is slightly warmer due to a mild westerly breeze.

River fishing brings back for me all the joys and delights of childhood, when the mystery surrounding the sport made me eager with anticipation. In chalk stream rivers you may well see either species take a hook-bait, the visual highlight of any fishing. With spate rivers you have to concentrate hard and have confidence in the swim you are fishing. The fish may be in front of you but will not feed or it may be closer in, further down, or further up. In clear water you can spot the fish, thus eliminating many of the unproductive areas. In coloured or tinged water you need to be experienced at reading the water to judge where the fish will lie, how you should approach them, and what time they will feed at.

To me, the delights of the river far outstrip the merits of big lakes and gravel pits. Something is always happening; the river is always flowing, going somewhere, carrying your bait to a waiting fish. I enjoy fishing the chub on a freeline, waiting for him to avidly grab the bait and then surge into the nearest snag on feeling the hook. But I like the barbel better; those orange fins, piggy little eyes, and that broad sweeping tail hiding unseen power. It is a majestic fish and a powerful fighter. My favourite technique for barbel is long trotting with a centre pin, floatfishing a cube of luncheon meat—utter bliss!

Still Water Fishing for Chub

I have already mentioned that chub fare better in still water than barbel and although my main concern in this book is to give you some advice about river fishing for both species, I think it is worth devoting a chapter to still water chub fishing. Presumably the age of still water chubbing came about because club secretaries became aware that many trout syndicates operated on stretches of game rivers that had no requirement for chub. With the cost of restocking coarse fish growing all the time, and limited availability on this species, fishing clubs thought it an ideal time to snap up any free offerings of fish. Sometimes game rivers discarded any netted or electro-fished coarse fish by dumping. Now they are more likely to offer them for sale, or give them to a club for nothing provided that they find them a home and arrange collection themselves.

With that sort of incentive many club waters suddenly became home to shoals of chub, and to the surprise of many anglers they were catchable. Soon after being stocked into a still water, the chub can be caught quite easily on conventional float or ledger rigs. In a river, when heavily fished, they can prove incredibly frustrating. The same problem soon arises in a still water, however, as the chub becomes wise to the fisherman's ploy. On initial stocking they will fall to floatfished or link-ledgered breadflake. As simple as that, just a huge piece of flake on a size 4 hook. After getting caught a couple of times however, or even seeing just one fish from the shoal being caught, they will retire to a safe sanctuary—a weedbed, overhanging trees, a gravel bar close to deep water, a bed of lilies or an island. The edge of an island is their favourite haunt, possibly stemming from their time as river fish when they frequently gravitated towards any sort of island. In a river, chub are known to be predatory, feeding on sticklebacks and minnows, particularly during the early months of summer when the minnows are in the process of spawning and less wary of predators. In still waters larger chub, over 3 or 4 lb, soon become aware of the first year fry of coarse fish, particularly roach and rudd fry. Some of the largest still water chub have been taken by anglers either pike fishing or eel fishing at night using a small, whole, dead fish for bait. You need plenty of patience for that sort of fishing and a liking for being out at first and last light. A 3 to 4-in. roach or rudd, threaded onto an 8-lb mono trace and a single size 2 hook is all you need. I like to fish with 12-lb trace if there is a chance of the bait being snaffled by an eel or small pike. If you use a wire trace you may still land a pike, but you're more likely to get a dropped run from a big chub. Stick to mono traces as you may only get one chance.

Just look at the size of a chub's mouth and you will see why they are capable of engulfing any size of hook-bait. At the back of the throat they have large pharyngeal teeth for crushing up food.

11

Go Fishing for Chub and Barbel

Taking advantage of their predatory instinct, you can take chub on lures. I must admit to never having caught one on a wobbling spoon, but they will take a bar spoon which is a lure with a blade that revolves around a bar when pulled through the water. Mepps and Veltic are about the best to go for and again, fish them on 8 to 12-lb line in case there are perch or small pike in the water. If you must weight the spinner for casting, put a swan shot about 2 ft up the trace so that it doesn't frighten the chub. This gives a helicopter effect when you cast but it shouldn't produce any tangles. When retrieving, many anglers make the mistake of twitching the rod top to supplement the action of the spinner but bar spoons have a vibratory as well as a visual effect and need to be retrieved smoothly and steadily. I picked up a useful tip from the mullet fishermen of Christchurch harbour that may also help here. They use a long, narrow bar spoon called a willow-leaf and tip a treble hook with an inch of ragworm for mullet. Nobody seems to know why mullet take the spinner but they do. Try tipping your hooks off with a couple of brandlings; it makes the chub grab harder rather than just nipping at it.

You can also use plugs to catch chub, the best in the pike angler's armoury being the mini 'S' from Shakespeare. I have had the most success with the mini and midi versions of this plug. For pike I twitch and jerk it hard but for the chub I keep it coming slowly and steadily. An alternative is to lip-hook a small, dead bait like a minnow and fish it freelined, retrieving in a sink-and-draw action. When the chub hits, drop the rod top for a second to allow him to turn the minnow then set the hook firmly. You should hook every one with this pause-strike method, something I learnt when fishing the Texas plastic worm rig for large-mouth bass on Florida's lake Okeechobee. Dead bait twitching like this is very much a roving affair and something to be tried when you're not exactly sure of the location of any shoaled chub. When you have located them, a dead minnow, freelined on the bottom near some weed, a bush or an island and bumped a foot every 30 seconds or so is great for a heavily-fished water. Make sure you keep close to the weed or relevant feature otherwise you will miss the fish.

The most entertaining method of bait fishing is undoubtedly surface fishing. The best period is in the stillness of first and last light

Still Water Fishing for Chub

The author took this fine net of chub on floaters—Pedigree Chum dog biscuits that have been soaked in water to make them expand to twice their size. They are a cheap and easy way of maintaining a constant flow of bait particles to encourage chub to feed on the surface.

and the most productive baits are cheap and easy to acquire. Floating casters are good when you know to within a few yards where the chub are located. They can usually be obtained from your tackle shop for nothing but the drawback is that they will also attract all the smaller roach and rudd. The alternative is to use Sugar Puffs, the breakfast cereal, which absorb water in about thirty seconds and are that much larger so will not be eaten by the fringe species. Casters are better in my opinion but the small fish can prevent the chub from getting a look in. By nudging and pushing but not eating the Sugar Puffs, the small fish may well just attract the chub over.

Approach the swim where you think the chub are from upwind, feeding in loose offerings of dampened Sugar Puffs so that the ripple carries them slowly down. This is better than using a long-range catapult to scatter the feed right onto the heads of the fish which is more than likely to frighten them. Instead of using a couple of Sugar Puffs on the hook for close range work, you may find a 1-in. square of crust from a loaf of bread will be taken just as well. This larger bait also avoids the ravages of the roach and rudd fry. Just hook the crust through twice, dunk it on the surface a couple of times so that it absorbs water and gives you some casting weight, then fire it out. A tip here is to leave a long drop from rod top to bait and cast softly, almost like throwing a paper dart into the air. Aim high and take it smoothly, otherwise you just find the crust flying off the hook. Once it settles on the surface it takes in more water and although you can generally move it to some degree, you will rarely get another cast from it. Better to hook on a fresh piece. If the chub are really finicky and mop up the loose offerings but ignore the crust you will obviously have to scale the size down and use either a single Sugar Puff or caster. Casting with so little bait weight is virtually impossible if the shoal is any distance from you, so why not use some Angler's Flotabait? This is a green, putty-like compound that can be squeezed around a plastic ledger stop about two feet from the hook-bait. Not only does it give you extra casting weight but it also acts as a visual marker during very windy weather. Another way to get a single Sugar Puff or floating caster out is to use a fly rod. I once fished in North Carolina for carp and although I got the fish to feed on giant-size Sugar Puffs, I couldn't get a hook-bait on them. The answer was a fly rod and long leader which shortly gave me some fish over 8 lb!

Ledgering for chub in a still water has never been one of my most successful techniques except when I've been using natural fish baits as described previously. You would think they would fall for maggots and swimfeeder techniques but they don't. The only way I have picked up the odd fish is by freelining luncheon meat to fish I have spotted cruising in shallow, weedy waters. You need to lead the fish by about five feet, depending on the water clarity, then as the bait sinks to the bottom and the chub follows it, wind in the tension and watch the bow in the line where it enters the water. Strike at the slightest twitch as chub in a lake are just as finicky as those in a river.

Right: The author in his own dinghy on Pangbourne Weir on the Thames. He is gently increasing the pressure with a high hand-hold to keep the chub away from a weedbed. Stop the chub from reaching its sanctuary and it should be yours.

Go Fishing for Chub and Barbel

Many of the club waters or day ticket venues now holding still water chub are heavily match fished. For that reason the fish are going to be on their guard when a lot of loose feeding is going in. Matchmen generally add some groundbait or cloudbait to attract the smaller roach and rudd so I would advise you to dispense with these and simply fire in the loose feed. Casters are probably the best for chub although they are expensive. You can actually draw the chub to the surface by feeding sinking casters and fishing 1 lb bottom, an 18 hook and bulk the shot under the float, using a single caster about 3-ft deep. If you start to miss a few, and the bites will be fast, start catapulting out the darker casters. They will be slower sinking and will therefore bring the chub nearer to the surface. Once you see them 'humping' just under the surface, use floating casters and drop the float about 1-ft down. The nearer the surface you can get them feeding, the better your chances of hooking one when you strike.

I have not heard of really big bags of still water chub being taken but generally you should be able to get two or three in a session. Just to summarise, my advice is that if you know the fish are recent stockings then lures and fish baits should catch them fairly easily but once the water gets fished more intensively, then you should resort to surface baits like casters or Sugar Puffs coupled with floating crusts. When the water gets really hard and you know there are some monster chub lurking there, use a small, dead fish ledgered or freelined on the bottom, as near to their haunts as you can get. Fish at dawn or dusk and you may be lucky and catch a monster fish. Unlike the barbel which is so perfectly designed to live in fast water, the chub is increasingly respected by clubs as a sought-after still water fish.

River Fishing for Chub

The chub is usually a most discerning river fish but occasionally it can seem very gullible, appearing to take anything thrown at it. This obviously makes it a popular fish with anglers. Hooked near the sanctuary of its home—generally a snaggy tree root, a weedbed or raft of rubbish—it can bend even a heavy rod. If it escapes to the snag, however, you can rarely get it out and much like the tench in a lily bed, it has an incredible knack of transferring the hook from its mouth to the snag. I have spent many minutes trying to free a chub that has long since gone, leaving my hook in the snag!

While the British record for this species is a little over 7 lb, there have been reports of record monster fish in years gone by—a 10 lb 8 oz fish in 1875 from the River Crane and an 8 lb 4 oz fish from the Hampshire Avon in 1913. On the continent, chub grow to almost 10 lb, presumably because of the higher temperature, and there was even a report of a $17^1/_2$-lb chub landed in the Ukraine. That's not the sort of fish you want to hook on a 2-lb line near a fringe of rushes. If there is such a thing as an 'average' fish, and much depends on locality, I would think in terms of about 2 lb.

The chub is a handsome fish with a large head and a white-lipped, cavernous mouth that is capable of tackling almost any size of coarse fish bait. Small chub are sometimes mistaken for large dace and the surest way to distinguish the two is to look at the leading edges of the dorsal, ventral and anal fins. On the dace they are concave, or curved in but on the chub they are convex, or curved out. The more you fish the more easily you will come to recognise the two. The dace has a far lighter olive-green back when seen in the water, while the chub has a dark edge to its tail fin. The colouring of the chub is fairly consistent and unlike other species the chub does not change its markings to suit its environment. It has a dark green, occasionally greyish-blue, back, with metallic bronze flanks and very large scales. In young fish the fins can have a tinge of red, especially in sizes of up to a pound in weight. The leading edge of the scales are lined with black, balancing the weave-effect scales in perfect symmetry.

These two youngsters are sharing a swim on a river having found a clear gap in the prolific high summer weed. The chub are likely to be in shoals under the weed so aim for these areas when casting out your bait.

While the chub likes fast-flowing gravel runs like the barbel, it is a much lazier fish and prefers to lie just on the edge of the current or at the trailing edge of a weedbed, where the current's pace is reduced. There it cruises, swinging out of position only to intercept a morsel of food. The barbel, in contrast is quite happy working in the fastest current. The only time you may see a large shoal of chub on a shallow, fast run is during spawning time. It is believed they are there to 'clean off' after spawning but close observation has indicated to me that they are spawning when on these runs. I say this because I have watched both dace, minnows and lampreys working directly below the chub and have seen them gobbling up free offerings which I assume must be eggs. I may well be wrong but the fact is that these chub will still take a bait in this fast, shallow water.

Chub breed from April to June, leaving sticky eggs deposited on stones or weedbeds, which hatch very quickly, in just over a week. At the time of spawning, the males, like Bream, develop tubercles and are rough to touch. Spawning times vary depending on the spring temperature. A cold, late spring and they will spawn into late June but a warm winter and spring will result in a much higher water temperature and spawning can be completed by the end of May. While I have seen large shoals of chub in the River Stour, Thames and Avon, most have been between 1 lb and 4 lb in weight. Once the chub get above 4 lb they tend to stay near their familiar features—tree roots, weed beds, rocks—in threes and fours. Very large chub may be entirely solitary fish except during the active spawning season. Although chub are widely distributed all over England, they are not found in any quantity in Wales, Devon, Cornwall or the north of Scotland.

Snaggy Swims

Years ago chub were a prime target in trout rivers, where it was believed they thrived to the detriment of the trout. Very often they were thrown out to rot but now, with a constant demand for fish by coarse angling clubs, most of the netted or electro-fished chub from trout rivers soon find another home in a club water. Chub fishing can be a serious affair if big fish are the quarry or it can be just a casual few hours at the riverside. Chub feed best during failing light and will often leave their snaggy homes to work over clear patches of gravel for food. It is this habit of living close to any snags that presumably led to Izaak Walton's description of the chub as 'the fearfullest of fishes'. They can stitch your line through a weedbed or tree root with

Go Fishing for Chub and Barbel

This swim on the River Kennet in Berkshire was impossible to fish from one side but Tackle Up shop manager, Nigel Newport, knew there were fish under the overhanging trees so he walked a mile round the fishery to tackle the swim from the other side. As you can see, he has perfect control of the bait and can steer it under the trees.

River Fishing for Chub

the skill of a professional weaver! The closer you can get your bait to one of these snags the better your chance of a take, especially when looking for fish over the 4-lb mark. Two baits of yesteryear were cherries or young mice with no hair. Presumably you had to remove the mouse from the mousetrap then whip over him quickly with a razor before consigning him to the river!

Assuming you have found a suitable swim you have to establish that the species is indeed at home. In clear water rivers this is easily done with the aid of polarising sunglasses and a hat with a wide peak on it. The glasses eliminate surface glare and allow you to see through the water better. If the fish can be seen your job is easy; if not, you are going to have to fish carefully. Let me also point out that this species has excellent eyesight and was once named the 'ghost' for its ability to fade way if frightened by a clumsy approach. A clumsy cast will also send the chub drifting away downstream into the nearest snag. Even if the swim looks ideal for ledgering, I suggest you run a float through first, which will be a lot less disturbing to the fish if done properly.

You are likely to be faced with two different paces of river current. On waters like the Hampshire Avon or Dorset Stour you may need an Avon-bodied float which allows you to use more weight for cocking it, which in turn means you have added stability in the heavier current. With all floats fixed top and bottom, you will want to hold the float back a little slower than the pace of the current. This is due to the fact that the river bed produces friction with the water and consequently the surface moves faster than the lower depths. If you use only a light float, the moment you 'mend' the line to hold the float back and thus allow the bait to precede it, your bait will drag round unnaturally. With a heavier float you can hold back quite hard without disturbing the pace of the bait below. Chub can be extremely wary of anything that doesn't travel down to them at the same pace as the river. Remember they inhabit the same few yards of water once they get over 3 lb and will be picking off drifting morsels all their lives!

For slower rivers like the Thames you can dispense with the heavy float and use a waggler. This is a float attached by the bottom end only and consequently it cannot be held back without pulling the float under and giving you a false bite. With this type of floatfishing you let the float run through unhindered as the water friction on the river bed will not be as pronounced as it is in a fast river.

Whichever pace of current you are dealing with, set up your position well upstream from the required swim. Throw in a few loose samples first, letting them run through with the current. Then bait up and cast out. One problem is that you will be unfamiliar with the depth of the swim you think the fish are in and any attempt to plumb it will destroy the fishing for the rest of the day. It is better to run the float through close to the surface on the first run, say two feet below and then add six inches to every subsequent run until you start catching the bottom. If the chub are at home you should get a take the first run through and if you haven't had a bite after about a dozen casts, I suggest moving to another swim.

The best tackle to use for this work depends largely on the type of sanctuary the chub are living near. If you have something substantial like tree roots or a raft of overhanging rubbish to contend with, then I suggest 5-lb line straight through to a size 6 hook and a big bait—either lobworm, cheese or bread. If you should hook a chub first cast, pile on the pressure and get him away from both the snag and possibly the rest of the shoal. If you fail to get a bite on the next couple of runs then you may need to put some extra feed in. Any chub hooked among a shoal will upset them all and you either need to leave them for an hour to let them regain confidence or pump in enough food to take their minds off worrying where their friend has just disappeared to! There is no need to pump in a load of feed straightaway when one fish on a single hook-bait will be considered a bonus. You also want to make sure the chub are in the area before you waste a whole lot of feed. Assuming you have no more bait, I suggest a mix of groundbait and a few samples of hook-bait. Throw the mix well upstream and after two or three balls have gone in, follow through as soon as possible with your hook and float. You should encourage the shoal to feed confidently and will maybe take another couple of fish. After that, no matter how much food you throw in, the shoal has begun to accept that the float travelling through the water with a suspended bait beneath it has something to do with the departure of its comrades. In addition their initial hunger has been satisfied somewhat by the food and with a partially full stomach, they are more likely to reveal that cautiousness they are renowned for.

This is the time to change to the ledger and anchor a big bait on the bottom to avoid the disturbing motion of the float continually passing through the water. With a fast current like the lower Stour or the Hampshire Avon you might need quite a bit of weight but do not overweight everything—use just enough weight to hold the bottom. You need to be able to cast as near to the upstream end of the swim as possible, avoiding disturbing the fish too much. Then, if you don't get a chub coming up out of the snag to pick up the bait, you can bump it back down to them by raising the rod top and dislodging the weight. You may also be limited in the length of 'tail' you can use, that is, the distance from the hook to the lead. If you have to drop the bait fairly accurately into a narrow run between a weedbed or a pool with boulders either side, then use a short tail. That means wherever the lead hits, the bait will be close to it. Using a long 'tail' in this situation could well mean that the weight reaches the bottom but the hook-bait gets caught up in the weed, out of sight of the fish, or worse still, ends up spinning and wobbling unnaturally in the current.

If, however, you have plenty of room directly upstream from the swim but have fish lying beneath, say, a raft of rubbish or overhanging willows, then you can use a long tail and bump that weight down towards the snag, confident that the hook-bait will be a good three feet under the snag itself. This way you are literally dishing it up on a plate right in front of them. The chub may respond by taking the bait within a few seconds of it settling on the bottom, or you may have to wait up to half an hour. Much depends on how frightened the fish have become and I have to warn you that no matter how careful you are, or even if you sit still for a full 30 minutes, they might not take at all. They are not completely stupid although their early-season feeding habits might suggest otherwise. They learn that a line running through the water means danger and the best way to put them at their ease is to leave the swim alone for an hour. You can either sit quietly on the bank or, like me, go off to try another swim.

I would say that the best chub bags I have ever taken were the ones when I hit maybe a dozen swims during one day, leaving each one

Go Fishing for Chub and Barbel

The more difficult the swim, the more likely it is that it will contain chub. Travelling light, scout a section of river first, mentally noting where you have seen fish. Here, Adrian Hutchins spots a fish discovered on a previous trip by the author. Adrian landed it first cast and later weighed it in at 5 lb!

Right: The smile says it all. A superb catch of chub taken by the author who watched and stealthily approached the fish. By carefully studying the chub you can often tell which fish from a shoal is likely to take your bait. These fish ran to well over 4-lb in weight.

after one or two fish, then returning to it later when it had quietened down. On many heavily-fished waters it can be fatal to stay in one swim and heap the feed in. The fish have learned to associate anglers with being caught and unless you have an excess of feed to give them, you are unlikely to bag up. It's much better to pick up the odd fish or two and then move on to pastures new, although the number of anglers fishing the water will dictate how far you can go.

Open Waters

Having dealt with snaggy swims, let's take a look at more open waters. One of the best places to find chub is at the upstream end of any island in weirpools. Contrary to popular opinion that the chub might be resting below the island, out of the force of the current, more fish will be caught at the upcurrent end and around the sides. I

have no explanation for this but I have caught plenty of chub fishing such places and I can only assume that food is funnelled by different currents through these areas. I once discussed this very point with a Thames trout angler in a weirpool. He believed that any insect floating down on the surface film would be sunk when that current hit the upcurrent end of the island and then carried down the sides under water where it was more readily available to the chub. Now why hadn't I thought of that?

Floatfishing such an area is only feasible by boat. You need to moor up about 10-20 yds upstream from the island and run the bait down to the swim using a bodied Avon float. There's no need for groundbait, just plenty of loose feed. When fishing from the bank you are going to be casting across the flow so you need to fish with a waggler float and cast to the head of the island, letting the float trickle round as close to the edge as possible. Invariably either wind or current will dominate the pressure on the line between rod top and float, causing some dragging of the float. To combat this you either take a chance and 'mend' the line with an upcurrent sweep of the rod or you let a touch more slack out. If you 'mend' the line you risk moving the float and the bait, thereby alerting the fish. If you let some line spill from the reel spool you will have a lot of slack to pick up on the strike. For this reason I advise facing downstream and striking horizontally rather than vertically. That way you keep all the line in the water and the drag of the line through the water on the strike will help to keep the hook in for that extra split second. Again, no loose feed, just your hook-bait for the first half a dozen runs through. Then add some loose feed and only when bites tail off again would I advise putting in groundbait.

Feeding

There may be an occasion when you think the fish are confined in a very small area. You then need to put in your feed with the aid of a swimfeeder. Chub love live food so use maggots whenever possible. To start with, use a block-end swimfeeder which dispenses maggots and not groundbait; then when bites tail off, use an open-ended feeder with a mix of groundbait and maggots. Once you have established a pattern and can identify the position of the first few casts, make sure you retain that accuracy as you want to keep all the feed as close as possible. When using a big bait you generally get a hard, confident take, but when you have small baits like maggots you

Winter on the upper River Avon. The author has waited all day for a bite from the fish he knows is there. Staying on until dusk gives you the best chance of catching a difficult fish.

can get tweaks and plucks which you may not think are chub. This happens on heavily-fished waters, when the fish know the swimfeeder means food but they also know picking up baits in its immediate proximity spells trouble.

In this situation you can try putting in more feed in an effort to relax the fish into a feeding mood again. On heavily-fished waters this can have an adverse effect however and actually push them out of the swim. A better idea is to lengthen the tail from hook to feeder—up to 3 ft. This means that for a while they lose the association of hook and feeder, which are likely to be used close together by other anglers. The problem here is that bite detection is not so sharp and the chub can pick up the small hook-bait and spit it out without you noticing at all! Strike at any tweak you get on the rod top. Another method is to scale down your tackle considerably. Instead of using, for example, a 4 lb line straight through, retain the main line but tie on a hook-link below the feeder of 2 lb or less, coupling it to a size 18 or 20 hook. If you are using maggots then put one on singly and you should get a few more fish. The problem with this is that when the chub are not hard into the swim, the other fringe species will move in. Roach, dace and minnows will swallow single maggots with ease and you get continuous bites from small fish. Every time you strike and wind in you will be disturbing any chub about to move up into the swim. Instead, try dropping down to small hooks and light tackle the moment the chub go off the feed as the smaller species will take some time to move into the swim.

If you start by using small hooks and links immediately you run the risk of hooking small fish and frightening any chub before they have had a chance to settle down. Only when you have felt a few chub and are confident that they are there but wary of feeding should you drop down to ultra-light tactics. It goes without saying that you shouldn't even contemplate going this light when fishing the snaggy swims for bigger chub.

The next type of water to consider is the main river area where there are no visible signs of any features such as roots, overhanging branches or islands. There may however be streamer weed with narrow channels in it and a clearer patch at the tail end of the weed. Chub are likely to be feeding in either of these areas and this is an ideal opportunity for using a lot of loose feed via a swimfeeder. The current may be faster than usual as a result of the constricting effect of the weedbeds and any loose feed will be whisked away if it is simply thrown in. One way round this would seem to be to throw the loose feed in much farther upstream than usual, allowing extra distance for sinking. The problem here is the variance of the currents caused by the many different channels between the weeds. One handful thrown accurately upstream may in fact split into three different channels and be whisked away from the fish. You need to get it hard down on the bottom, close to the fish, but without casting too close so as to frighten them.

By treading carefully, you can move right out to where the chub live. This is especially advisable in summer when they seldom leave the weed until dark. Here an angler is floatfishing maggots in a tiny run between two beds of streamer weed.

Go Fishing for Chub and Barbel

In my own experience chub do not respond well to heavy groundbaiting. They are undoubtedly attracted into the areas but by watching them carefully I have observed that they ignore the groundbait and go straight for the primary loose feed, whether it is maggots, caster or sweetcorn. Two of the best baits for holding chub in a swim are casters and hempseed although I must emphasise that the latter should be properly cooked. Mix together hemp and caster, then use either a single caster or maggot on the hook, with hemp and caster in the feeder. When you cast out, wait no longer than 3 or 4 minutes before you refill and cast again. The idea is to lay down a constant trail of loose feed, allowing the current to wash it down to the waiting chub. Once they are alerted, they mop up all the loose feed and work their way upcurrent to the area around the feeder and your waiting hook.

It is worth mentioning that some shop-bought feeders do not empty quickly enough. I suggest you drill slightly larger holes so that those tempting seeds escape more quickly. This sort of fishing should only be done in conjunction with a quivertip which allows you to see the bites in fast water, as opposed to a standard rod top which will be too stiff. If you can afford to put in plenty of casters you will find the chub getting so engrossed in feeding, that they won't become scared of the feed hitting the water. This was illustrated to me many years ago when the use of maggots on the famed Royalty Fishery of the Hampshire Avon was in its heyday; all the fish from a length of river grouped together, waiting for their daily feed. At that time the cost of a day ticket on this prime stretch of river was about £1.50 and a gallon of maggots cost just £3. Needless to say, the most successful anglers were those throwing the most maggots which in turn meant other anglers followed suit until at least a gallon of maggots was being thrown in to every one of the top swims every day throughout the summer and autumn. With that sort of intensive feeding most fish lose all sense of caution, despite being caught, and await the bombardment of bait at about 8 am! You used to be able to stand up and swing out either a swimfeeder or a baitdropper and the chub would actually mill around waiting for the 'dinner bell' to ring as the bait came in. They would even cluster around a baitdropper trying to knock it open. I tried to capitalise on this myself when fishing the famous 'pipes' swim. By midday in June and July you could see every fish in the swim so I rigged up the baitdropper on a link of nylon, tied on a hook-link, baited up and swung it out. Sure enough the chub raced around trying to knock the baitdropper open and I managed to take several fish before I discovered my major design fault. The line occasionally got cut as the brass lid swung open and it was also difficult to detect bites as barbel kept banging into the line! Those fish were just waiting to be fed and while this was many years ago, it is still worth remembering that given enough feed chub, along with other fish, lose all their caution. Nowadays, with maggots over £10 a gallon and a day ticket almost as much, the chances of a return to that frenzied style of feeding are remote.

Heavily feeding a swim with hemp and caster is likely to keep the fish preoccupied but they can also get extremely picky and will often not take more than a single caster. Short of scaling down your hook and link size, which in turn puts the odds in favour of the fish snagging, there is little you can do except wait. Put in half a dozen casts with an open-ended feeder, filling it full with hemp, casters or maggots but plugging the end loosely with a cap of soft groundbait. You can empty the feeder by waiting 30 seconds for the groundbait to soak, then give it a sharp strike and the contents should empty out in one go. When you have done this half a dozen or a dozen times, depending on how much bait you can afford, just sit back and leave it to settle.

As in the snaggy swim situation, the chub associates the splash of a feeder hitting the water both with feed and a need to be cautious. They want the feed but don't want to get hooked, so they take their time moving up the swim to pick off free offerings. They leave anything that doesn't look quite right and are completely uncatch-able. What you must do is sit back for half an hour, or go for a walk, maybe chubbing another swim, letting them regain their confidence in feeding. They are, after all, essentially greedy fish and soon start feeding hard, especially if they are in competition with a shoal of smaller, more gullible chub. When you return to the swim, you should take at least another chub or two before they again get cautious. They will only respond to this resting technique two or three times and then you have to wait until failing light conditions

give them the confidence to feed hard. The problem is that you think they are not touching your bait but in fact they can pick up a caster and shell it or pop it, then spit it out without your quivertip registering a bite. Far better to rest the fish for a while and then get a strikeable bite when you return.

Fast Waters

In faster, deeper waters such as weirpools, rapids and bends I don't advise using small baits at all. In fact I rarely fish a float on such turbulent waters as you end up striking at false bites. This is the place for the experienced ledger fisherman. The modern quivertip rods are so sensitive that I think they are just as successful in the right hands as a float. I see no point in using more than one rod as the rod should be an extension of your arm, a piece of fishing equipment with which you feel completely at home. These are two methods that I would advise for fishing fast, deep waters for chub. You can either fish a static bait on the bottom or you can roll it around, searching out all the likely places using the power of the current. While many of the fish will move through the most turbulent water as it pours into the pool, they will be cruising rather than feeding. In all weirpools there is a pocket of slack water immediately before the actual torrent that gushes through and it's here that a large bait ledgered in what at first appears to be a stupid position, can result in one or two fish. It's an area usually ignored by most anglers but take my word for it there are pockets of quieter water in this region where the fish do go.

The next best place to fish is in the eddy where the current back-pedals into the main surge. Don't make the mistake of fishing facing downstream from the main surge. In this situation the current will roll the lead around until it finds a spot to rest but the bait will roll round towards you meaning any fish picking up the bait is likely to come into contact with the main line first. Smaller chub take no notice and often bolt down the bait as soon as they see it but larger chub are a little more wary. You need to move to a position slightly

Left: Never neglect even the smallest weirpool in the height of summer. Chub love to feed where the oxygen content is at its highest and a weir sill is just such a place.

round the side of the weirpool which allows you to face downstream to the eddy flow, not into it. Then any chub picking up the bait is less likely to come into contact with the line first and you get a more positive bite.

Another place to try is among the pilings at the sides of the weir where the current is deepest. The chub often lie six inches out from any pilings and I like to run the float through first just to see if anyone is at home. Generally it dips on the first run through but this piling or undercut bank area is often home to the smaller chub of up to 1 lb or so. The fight will undoubtedly put off any larger chub, so much depends on whether you are satisfied catching small chub. For larger chub, fish parallel to the bank and use a long tail from weight to hook. The faster current will put tension on it and straighten it out, so you get a good bite. Do not just stand over the top of the bank edge you want to fish and lower the bait down. For one thing the fish is likely to see you but for another, the pressure from the heavy current will put a bow in the line from rod top to ledger weight and being in a downstream curve this may mean it hangs out over your hook-bait more. If the chub doesn't see the line it may well bump into it and frighten itself. This is another reason why I advise using a fairly long hook-link, for example 3 ft, in order to keep the bait well away from the main line. A small point but on a hard winter's day it could mean the difference between a fish hooked and a fish lost!

Of all the areas in a weirpool, the tail end of the pool where the current splits away, is generally recognised as the best place. Now I shall let you in on a little secret. Most anglers think the best place to put the bait is in the main channel as the power of the initial surge fades and the current channels into the main flow of the river. I can see the reasoning behind this, as all the food should be funnelled through here. However, as it rushes over the weir, the churning water goes down, hits the river bed and shoots up again towards the surface. This gives rise to the many boils and swirls you see, particularly where the bottom is uneven. Any loose food particles will also be churned up towards the surface but being slow to sink, they may not hit the bottom again for some distance downstream. Some of the food and insects go straight down this main flow but remain high in suspension in the water, not near the bottom. The food that is

River Fishing for Chub

Essex angler Jerry Airey returns a good chub straight after catching it.

swirled around in the eddies, however, is circulated for longer and even after being churned upwards, it will fall towards the bottom before the main channel of flow and drop away to the sides. Therefore, placing a bait to either side of the main tail flow, rather than directly in it, puts the food where it would naturally fall, and where chub (and barbel) are likely to congregate.

There will still be a 'hotspot' where the chub will be taking even better. Most weirpools have a shallower area at the tail end of the pool where winter flood water has pounded out the gravel in a churning action and deposited it at the back of the pool. Most weirpools will have this bank of gravel or even an island in the centre of the pool but the flow around that island or gravel bank will not be of equal power. The main current will invariably flow to one side, leaving a larger eddy on one side of the pool than the other. With a

35

larger eddy, the amount of food churned around and therefore sinking to the bottom will be greater and naturally the fish learn this. Chub should be found at the tail end of the pool but slightly to the edge of the main flow on the side with the largest eddy.

A final suggestion for locating the chub is to return to the main eddy and detect where the eye of the eddy is situated. This will be the area of least turbulence and the place where food will be sinking to the bottom quicker. It is similar to the eye of a hurricane—in the centre the air is calm but the further out you go, the stronger the wind power. Apply the same principles to a weirpool eddy and you will have found one of the few places where it is possible to hold a float for chub. On small rivers and streams this is easy as a long, 13-ft match rod will hold the main line high off the water and out of the flow. In a large weirpool you have to resort to a ledger.

For ledger fishing on any of these holding areas I would advise a swan-shot link ledger held on a short link by a plastic ledger stop. You can then slide the lead up and down the main line in order to

In fast water, try to keep the rod top high when using a quivertip and ledger in order to minimise the water drag on the line.

shorten or lengthen the hook length without damaging the line. It is also easy to take off or add weight to suit the different areas you cast to. When fishing a big bait up under the flow from a weir sill or in an eddy as described you may need an ounce or more of lead. When you roll your bait around at the tail end of a pool you want only enough lead to bump bottom, with the bait finally coming to rest where the current lets it. Keep your rod tip as high up out of the current as possible but not so high that you have no striking power left or fall off your chair because the rod goes too far back! Try to use one rod with a 2-oz quivertip and get used to the trembles and tweaks from the bait clipping stones as it bounces around.

The bite, when it comes, may be a kick back of the tip, releasing it from tension, then a couple of hard jabs down. Once you become familiar with the technique you learn to strike as soon as the bow in the tip straightens and of course, the use of a heavier lead to firmly anchor the bait should leave you in no doubt as to what a bite looks like. The only problem can be the dragging of the tip when bits of weed and debris hit the line. I have seen anglers using two rods when water rules allow and I do so myself when the fishing is hard.

Touch-Ledgering

Once you start to get bites you should put away the rod and touch-ledger for maximum efficiency. This involves holding the rod with the line in front of the reel being looped across your finger, much like crooking your finger around the trigger of a gun. When darkness comes and you cannot accurately see the bites on the quivertip, you can feel the plucks on that finger. I like to go one step further and hold the rod with my right hand but use the third finger on my left hand to hold the line in front of the reel. The reason for this is quite simple. I am right handed, so all the skin on the balls or tips of my fingers are hard on that hand. The left hand gets used less so the skin is not so hard and consequently more sensitive to tension on the line. The third finger is also used least and therefore very soft compared, for example, with my right index finger which has tied so many hooks and removed so many trebles when piking that it's as tough as leather!

Another tip of mine you might like to try is licking the ball of your third finger immediately after every cast before holding it over the line at an angle. A wet finger sticks to the line better and therefore lets you know the split second a fish has picked up the bait. I also like to bump the bait an inch or so every minute not only to ensure the bait isn't stuck in weed but also to acclimatise that wet third finger to the bump of the bait on the stones.

Freelining

My favourite method of taking chub in clear rivers where visual location is easier is by freelining. This involves no weights, floats or other encumbrances on the line—just a hook and bait. On a good day, given bright sunshine that allows me to see the fish, I can achieve a very high success rate, even when other anglers are struggling with standard bait methods. You begin to develop an awareness for the fish. You know, as soon as the bait hits the water, whether they are going to take it or ignore it. The best bait for me is undoubtedly cheese. No need for fancy, strong flavours; ordinary mild, English cheddar will do the trick. In summer you need to keep your block of cheese cool otherwise it sweats and is too soft for bait. Remember you have no weight other than the bait and when casting a freelined bait you need to sweep the cast through the air much wider than usual.

To keep all of your baits cool—and your lunch and drinks for that matter—I suggest buying an ASW Coolfishbag in the smallest size. They take blue freezer blocks and have an inner lining sleeve to separate the bait or food from the blocks. For carrying bait when wading and fishing on the move, I use a kangaroo-style pouch that hangs around my neck on a cord. It's easy enough to make your own. Keep your main 1-lb block of cheese in the ASW bag, then break a piece off and wrap it in a piece of tinfoil and place it in the pouch

Right: Freelining a bait for chub in a river demands lightning reflexes. Nevertheless, many fish are just lightly lip-hooked like this big Dorset chub being unhooked by the author.

when you are off looking for chub. When you run out go back and get some more fresh bait.

In the weirpools you can use freelined cheese but the power of the

Using Mukluk chest waders, the author can wade out and fish a float directly between the gravel runs in the streamer weed for barbel or chub.

current on the line, rather than the bait, will keep it running high, too high for the chub and too 'dull'. You need to get in downstream of where you want to cast using either chest waders or thigh waders. (Ever since I got hold of a pair of Mukluk chest waders for my bass fishing expeditions, I have gone right off thigh waders as the extra depth available gives me more confidence to wade fast water like weir pools.) Having positioned yourself downstream from the fish, overcast the area but as soon as the bait hits the surface engage the reel and wind in, just keeping contact with the bow in the line. You don't want any slack lying on the surface. This keeps the water pressure to a minimum on the line, allowing the bait to sink at a more natural speed. As an added precaution, I also suggest you wind the line across the second and third fingers of the hand holding the rod. With the line running between these fingers you will immediately pick up the extra taps and tweaks that indicate the fish has picked up the cheese on its free fall. Once the bait hits the bottom, the tension will be evident on the line and the tip will bend over.

I did have some problems trying to cast a freelined bait when using a rod with either a spliced in or screwed in quivertip. This was particularly apparent on rainy or misty days, when moisture collecting in the tiny quivertip rings created a drag factor which made the cast drop too short. Casting harder merely caused the cheese to fly off. For this reason, you may have to re-ring the quivertip using larger rings so that moisture doesn't collect in them. A small point but good fishing techniques develop from paying attention to such details.

When the freelined bait comes into contact with the gravel, the tip either bends over as the current pulls on the line, or tweaks erratically as the bait bumps along. In the former instance I like to leave the bait under tension for at least a minute. If a chub intercepts it he releases the pressure on the quivertip and it springs straight. Don't wait for the tip to pull over again as it would do in the conventional bite registration when downstream fishing. If the tip springs straight it's because the chub has picked the bait up – he isn't going to hang on to it for ever, so strike the moment the tension comes off. Alternatively, when a freelined cheese bumps along the gravel the quivertip tweaks about, looking like a bite but you must judge the size of each tweak and then strike at anything that looks sharper. Judging this type of bite registration will depend on experience; a small chub will make the tip tweak sharply several times and will, like small, gullible fish of any species, hang on to it longer. With a bigger chub you get the one strong bite and that's it. You either nail him then, or miss him completely.

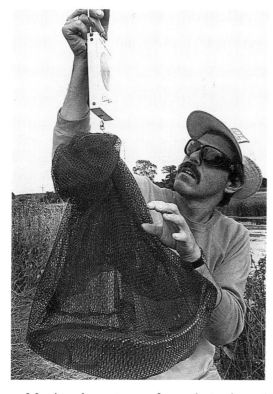

The author weighs a big chub to see if it makes the magic 5 lb mark. This Throop chub was a few ounces short, but it is still a noteworthy fish by any standards.

Moving downstream from the weirpool there are two methods of fishing the main river where the flow is quieter but still regular. The first involves concentrating on the naturally slack area behind a weedbed, or on the inside or back end of a bend, or behind a boulder. This will be a slightly slower area and a good holding place for chub. Again, you come up against the problem of water pressure on the line but to a lesser degree. Position yourself as close as possible to the swim, about 45 degrees across from the fish. Cast out upstream, and try to feather the spool lip to make the bait swing slowly into the pocket of slower water. With luck it should rest on the bottom. The tension will become evident on the rod tip and it is advisable to place the rod in a rest to keep the tip tensioned evenly. By watching for the bite you should be able to strike the fish easily. The second method is to keep a close eye on the line where it enters the water. Ideally you need still conditions to do this for there will always be a slight bagging of the line from the top of the rod to the water's surface. Once it has come under tension with water pressure it is extremely sensitive to the bite. Often the bow in the line starts to straighten a second before the quivertip registers the bite and it is therefore ideal when you are fishing failing light conditions at dusk.

If you can see chub, either in a shoal or individually, at the tail of a run and in shallow water, you need to try to attract them with a naturally flowing bait, from a distance. Do not get too close. Drop your cheese into the water on a line that will run it down naturally to them. If the cheese hits the bottom before it reaches the chub, you should keep the rod top high and gently tweak it up again, holding back a little to send the cheese down to the chub. This is one of the most exciting ways of catching chub, and you need cool nerves and a good reflex action in your wrist to hit them. If the chub ignore the bait, letting it go past them almost unnoticed, or if they drift disinterestedly under the weed, you need to dispense with the freeline and put on a link-ledger. Fix the weight about 10 in. from the hook, use a couple of swan shots, cast down towards where the fish were, and *do not* take your eyes off the cheese! In anything from half a minute, to little more than five minutes, a chub should appear at the tail of the swim and once he locates the source of the smell drifting towards him he will work up towards the bait. If confident, he will scoff it straight away and you should set the hook. If finicky, or wary of being hooked, he is going to play tag and give you a frustrating time.

A chub can confidently move up to a piece of cheese, stop dead 2 inches in front of it, tip its head down and nuzzle the cheese with those big white lips. Many is the time I have struck because those lips obscured the bait and my nerves couldn't stand it any longer. Chub can also pick up a cheese bait in their lips and just hold it lightly.

River Fishing for Chub

There is no choice but to strike and of course all you do is miss the fish as the hook tears out of the bait. If you do hook him it will only be a fringe hooking which invariably tears out when you apply pressure to stop the fish escaping to its sanctuary. I once made a rig which I nicknamed 'the hair in reverse'. The hair rig was devised by carp anglers as a means of presenting a bait with the hook outside the bait, tied to the bend with a 'hair' link of 1-lb line or less. My rig consisted of squeezing the cheese around a plastic ledger stop about half an inch above the hook. With the current acting on the hook it would lie an inch downstream from the cheese. When picked up by a 'lippy' chub the hook was farther back in the mouth and at least gave me a good hookhold.

If you fish rivers where you are not able to see the fish, you can still

On slow, deep stretches of river, both chub and barbel will come to the float. It is an exciting method and requires far more tackle control than ledgering.

Left: A good chub on the bank, taken on a favourite bait, cheese. Squeeze the cheese a couple of times and mould it onto the hook—there is no finer chub bait.

adopt all of these techniques with success but you need to keep your eye trained either on the quivertip or on the bow of the line where it enters the water. A fascinating method of fishing is to loose feed maggots, building the fish up into a feeding frenzy, then trying to catch them on the float. Chub are one of the hardest species to take once they become familiar with a particular size of bait. Many anglers will be familiar with the problem. You loose feed maggots, get the chub taking them, hit a couple on the float, then . . . nothing! The fish are still there and ready to take loose feed as fast as you catapult it in. The problem, however, is that even if you run your float through a cloud of loose-fed maggots, those chub gulp down every maggot except the one on the hook.

The situation always seems worse on a sunny day when you can see a swim still black with feeding chub, taking every maggot except yours. If you are fishing a deep swim close by a snag you can catch chub by using a 13-ft match rod. All you are trying to do is to freeline a single maggot using, for example, a size 18 hook and 2-lb line. The first problem is trying to get the maggot to sink in the current as naturally as the loose feed. It's lighter and any down-stream or upstream wind will cause it to drag unnaturally. All you need do is pinch a number 4 shot onto the main line about 12-15 in. from the bait. This enables you to control the bait more easily. If the chub are behind a clump of floating rubbish or a raft of weed under the bank at your feet and the wind is very strong, pinch on a swan shot about 3 ft from the hook. You can then swing out the bait, lower the lot to sink naturally until the swan shot is touching the surface and combat the wind. A useful tip for windy days.

Fly Fishing

If the chub are taking loose feed farther out in the river and you cannot stretch out with a match rod, use a fly rod. I first used this method on the Hampshire Avon during the boom period of the late Sixties when a cluster of maggots sent both chub and barbel completely wild. I use a size 18 hook or smaller for a maggot otherwise the action of casting folds the maggot into the bend of the hook and makes it look unnatural. Adding a second maggot after threading the first up and over the spade end knot produces a twist in the hook-link which again looks unnatural. You need to use a floating line and a short leader of about 8 ft. Striking can be a problem and it is difficult to describe on paper. Rather than trying to pick the line off the surface to set the hook, I find it better to strike sideways using the suction of the surface film on the line to pull the hook in. Certainly you miss some fish but you are also going to catch a few that you never would have seen if you had not used a fly rod.

On the subject of fly rods, it is perhaps worth mentioning that you can take chub and barbel on artificial flies. The Victorian method of dapping a live bluebottle on the surface using a long rod is, of course, likely to be more successful, but I feel most anglers would feel happier using an artificial fly. I now have a confession to make—I have only taken a handful of chub by fishing a wet fly under the surface. They definitely respond better to dry flies and will also take nymphs well, particularly in small streams. The chub is not a great fan of the extensive contents of a trout fisherman's fly wallet. He has no desire to learn all the Ephemerida family; he doesn't worry if it's a dun, a spinner, an upwinged fly, a spent or whatever. If it looks edible he'll take it! For that reason I use only large, black, fuzzy, dry flies, like the Grannom, which is a great chub catcher. The fish will still rise well to a smaller dry fly, as used for trout, but the small hook has less of a hold on the fish as it tries to escape to the sanctuary of the tree roots. The advised patterns are on traditional lines favouring flies like the Zulu, with its red tag and black fuzzy hackles. The Palmer, a large brown fly has either a red or white tag to its stern. Almost any pattern of white moth will do, particularly in dusky conditions when you want to see where your fly is on the shiny surface.

The problems of striking will be familiar to trout fishermen. Remember to pause to let the chub turn down, before picking the line off the surface in a firm striking action. Remember too that you are using a fly rod which has considerably less stopping power than the traditional Avon ledger rod. Don't be afraid to put the brakes on as soon as you can otherwise the chub will bore through one weedbed and out the other side. When fishing a nymph below the surface you can give it a few tweaks to attract the chub's attention. Where a trout may shy away, a chub will often swim straight over and take it. I have no idea if there is a really successful method for sunk-line fishing for chub in the deeper parts of a river. As I freely admit, I have only ever taken a handful on traditional wet flies. To my mind, fly fishing is not the most successful way to take chub, it is merely an alternative.

Surface Fishing

With regard to surface fishing, I should tell you about floating baits. Crusts of bread drifted down the gravel shallows early in the season are sure to bring the chub up. All you need is the same freelining rod mentioned earlier but you may have to grease about 20 ft of your main line nearest to the hook. Once the line sinks below the surface film it will drag and reduce the speed of the crust on the surface. Anything that doesn't look entirely natural is going to be ignored by

Judging by the wear on its tail fin, this big River Stour chub has been caught several times. Keep your fish in the net for the shortest possible time or, better still, catch and release them singly. Note the large head of this fish—a sign of the stomach larva or parasite that keeps the fish's weight down.

A pair of superb chub lying alongside the traditional Alcock's Aerial centrepin reel. Specimens like these landed by the author are well within the capabilities of most anglers.

Above: If the river is wide and you find float control difficult—perhaps because of downstream winds—wade out and set up stall mid-river where you can control your tackle better and present a bait to the chub without making them wary.

Below: Link ledgering a large lobworm on the gravel shallows in high summer brings rewarding results. The author slides a 3-lb chub over his net, taking it from the shallows above the boathouse swim on the Royalty Fishery at Christchurch.

An impressive catch of chub from Throop Fishery with some fish weighing over 4 lb. They all fell to freelining tactics—the author struck as he saw the chub's lips closing around his cheese hook-bait. There is an art to freelining and the author has taken bags of up to 80 lb by learning the skill.

Above: A black buzzy fly fished on the surface is most successful when fly fishing for chub.

Left: A big five pounder! The author with a magnificent winter River Stour chub taken, surprisingly, on a piking session near Hampreston. The fish fell to a big 'S' plug fished beneath willow trees confirming that the species do have predatory instincts.

One of the best ways to tackle a finicky chub is with a quivertip. Here Nigel Newport tries to outwit a shoal of chub on the River Kennet that refused all offerings and ignored all other tactics.

Above left: Chub do take sweetcorn but they can become very difficult on this bait. Perhaps the bright gold colour makes them wary and it may be better to fish this bait after dark.

Above right: A well-stocked bait tray ensures you can ring the changes with finicky chub and eventually find something they will take.

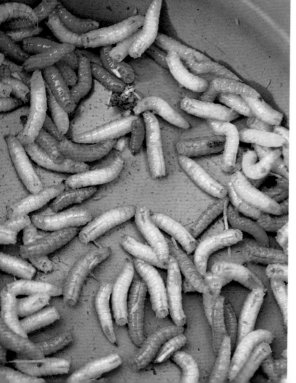

Left: Many matchmen prefer coloured maggots to plain white maggots. In the author's experience it is not the colour but the number you can put in that will make the difference.

The snaggier the swim the better. Here an angler hits into a Thames fish after wading out in chest waders to run his float tackle past the hulls of some moored boats.

The author admires a Throop chub that just reaches the magic 5-lb mark. In small, overgrown streams a 2-lb chub can be a good catch so judge your results accordingly.

the chub. Set up a pattern of crusts floating in a line, flicking them out and not casting until the chub have started to take them. Pedigree Chum mixer dog biscuits are even better than bread crusts. Used primarily by carp anglers, the trick is to soak them for a short while, then drain them and leave them to swell. As they absorb water they become soft and expand to twice their original size. You can even flavour them if you wish, using any one of the numerous colourings and flavourings now available at your local tackle shop. If you need extra casting weight, use a piece of green Flotabait on a plastic ledger stop about a foot from the bait. It also floats well, giving you a good warning of a take. Pedigree Chum Mixer biscuits are also very cheap so you can loose feed plenty of them in the water. Surface baits like this are best used in the early summer months of the season when the chub will be in the shallows after spawning, moving about more in the higher water temperatures. Chub fishing can be exciting and offers the angler a wide variety of different techniques. This relatively easy-to-catch species, will draw on all your watercraft skills for no species, except perhaps the mullet, can drift away like a ghost at the slightest mistake.

Tackle Suggestions

I see no point in giving separate information about tackle for chub and barbel as you are going to hit either of them by using the same techniques and baits, possibly even in the same swim on consecutive casts. The only real difference is the need to step up your tackle rating if you are interested in very big barbel from either a heavily snagged or weeded swim. I would advise stepping up line strengths to at least 8-lb breaking strain; no hook links of weaker line. Just one plastic ledger stop for a sliding weight link and a hook. Use a rod like a $1^3/4$-lb test-curve carp rod and centrepin reel. The extra power of the rod will be appreciated once you have hit a big barbel over 8 or 9 lb in weight and more pressure can be applied using a centrepin than a fixed spool. This only sounds like a minimal increase but it's worth noting if you have big barbel lined up in a particular type of swim.

Rods

For standard floatfishing for chub and barbel you need look no farther than a regular carbon or carbon glass mix 13-ft float rod. From this you can work a 4-lb line straight through or drop down to 2-lb hook-links or less if the fish are cagey and you are only using single maggots. I have taken barbel on match rods but they are certainly not made for barbel fishing, as you will no doubt find out! A

Before he knew better, the author would use every conceivable rod, reel and bait to tackle the Royalty Fishery for barbel. Now he rarely fishes with more than one rod and moves swims constantly until he locates the fish.

Go Fishing for Chub and Barbel

The author fights a fish hooked on a balsa float and centrepin reel on the famous Throop fishery of the Dorset Stour. Floatfishing a cube of luncheon meat is deadly here.

Ryobi quivertip $1^1/4$-lb test-curve Avon rod has two tips (a quivertip and a plain tip), and will set you up for any floatfishing expedition for chub and barbel.

You may suffer from 'line-stick' with the quivertip rings when freelining so use the other standard section when floatfishing. At 11 ft in length it is ideal for 'mending' the line on its journey downstream and the carbon content ensures you have an immediate response on the strike. I personally would like to see Ryobi bring out a $1^1/2$-lb test-curve rod in the same design, as the rod may be just a shade light for catching 5 to 8-lb barbel. I have done it, but that extra power would come in handy to stop a fish.

Reels

For applying pressure on either a chub or a barbel there is nothing better than a good centrepin. If possible, get your hands on an old Rapidex or Alcocks Aerial. They take a bit of mastering when it comes to casting but they can give a great deal of pleasure when playing a fish, or when running a float a long way down the swim, a method called 'long trotting'. They should be so finely balanced that they give line to the float in moving water without any assistance from your hands. I'm afraid my own models have seen better days and are full of sand and old oil. It's one of the jobs I really must get round to!

The fixed spool is much easier and there are a variety of models in the tackle shops. The best range, in my opinion, is the Shimano range. They operate smoothly and have stern drags. If you can, get hold of a good second hand model—the old ABU Cardinal 541s were excellent and adequate for big barbel as well. I still use mine although that too requires a little maintenance. The problem with being an all-round fishing writer is that there are no slack periods between species; consequently tackle maintenance tends to take a back seat.

With the stern drag models you have several of the Ryobi range to choose from. These are competitively priced and offer two of the models ideally suited for every eventuality when barbel and chub fishing. The Mastermatch MM300 is a shallow-spooled, open-faced float reel with a manually operated bale arm. This has the advantage of having a shortened reel stem which enables the finger controlling the flow of the line to reach the lip of the spool quite easily. It features

Using a centrepin reel for the control of float tackle is a traditional but difficult method. It can be pleasant to use but you will need a heavily-loaded float in a fast current just to get the hang of it. A centrepin is excellent for playing big fish.

a lightweight carbon spool with good line laying, so each trot down with the float should be clean and without jerks. This reduces the chance of line-bedding when you play a fish in under pressure. It has a particularly good rapid retrieve system, around 33 in. of line regained for every turn of the handle. With a silent anti-reverse and a positive feel it is good for both chub and barbel on the float. For ledgering, the Mastermatch ledger has many of the same features but has a much deeper spool to allow larger line capacities. The MM300 gives 100 yards of 2.5-lb b.s. line, while the Mastermatch ledger gives an option with 100 yds of 6 lb, 250 yds of 12 lb, 190 yds of 15 lb or 140 yds of 20 lb. I see no reason to go much above 8 lb and that is only required when fishing for big barbel near heavy weedbeds or snags.

What a disgusting creature! Not the author, but this 2-ft long lamprey that normally attaches itself to the flank of a salmon and then, using its sharp teeth, proceeds to eat the salmon away. It is a parasite and is often destroyed by salmon enthusiasts.

Tackle Suggestions

Lines

Almost every experienced angler will have a good reason for using a particular brand of line and I suppose I am no different. For years I have used Maxima, mainly for its supple quality and minimum visibility when in the water. The only drawback is that once it starts to get a few scuffs and nicks from rubbing on weedbeds or stones, it can break without warning. Don't make the mistake of peeling off a few yards, snapping it and thinking you are back on good line. Scrap the lot and spool up again, otherwise you are going to lose a good fish on it. The American line, Ande, is also highly rated and the 4-lb category has had several world-record gamefish taken on it. I use the 4-lb for light tackle saltwater fishing so it should certainly be up to the mark for freshwater use. For making up hook-links with small hooks for maggots and casters use Bayer. It comes highly recommended by match anglers and I have had few problems with it. Drennan line is also quite good for hook-links.

Hooks

There are thousands of different hooks on the market and it is really up to each individual to decide which hooks produce the best results. Some hooks are so specialised that they are not suitable for freshwater fishing. In the smaller hooks range, from a 12 down to an 18, I don't think any one brand stands out—the points are so small that even a basic pattern will be quite sharp. In the larger sizes, required for big baits such as cheese, luncheon meat or worms, sharpness should be at the top of your list. If you don't care to sharpen your own with a stone every time you go fishing, I suggest you start to look at the chemically sharpened hooks. They really are sharp although a watchful eye should be kept on the points when floatfishing. A lot of the time you may well be striking stones, branches or snags and if the hook hits these the point can be slightly bent over. If you don't take the trouble to check carefully, your next fish may stay on a second and then come off! Last season I started to use a range of hooks that impressed me greatly. Although the wire was a little thick, Partridge Specialist hooks from Alan Bramley at Redditch were a real pleasure to use. I first noticed an increase in hooking rate down on the Dorset Stour where I was freelining for chub. Early in the season you miss few fish as the bites are confident but once other anglers crowd in on the same water you tend to miss quite a few. Over three sessions of using Partridge hooks I hardly missed a fish and while I would be delighted to put this down to an increase in my own angling skill, I have to say it must have been those hooks! I followed this up with sessions fishing small to medium sized carp on a water that is famous for its twitchy bites. Again, the very high percentage of bites could only be attributed to the sharpness of the hook points.

Floats

Floats should always be of the best quality. I used to make some floats out of reeds but found they became waterlogged and sank very, very slowly! I learnt that good floats are not easy to make and I now stick to the shop-bought variety. For waggler fishing use bodied wagglers and get the larger sizes so that you can use an extra shot with them. This allows you a bit more leeway in line drag on windy days. The same applies to bodied Avons. Get them in a variety of sizes and never be afraid to shot a large float right down to the tip. When long trotting with a big bait like luncheon meat you are going to be holding back quite hard anyway which will make the float rise up a quarter of an inch.

Swimfeeders

You have several swimfeeders to choose from. The open-ended variety are intended for use with groundbait mixes or for putting a lot of loose feed in quickly. Plug both ends with groundbait and fill the middle with loose feed. You can also get a feeder called a block-end

On the bottom is the 'coffin' feeder, a meshed frame that was popular in the late 1960s when maggots were cheaper and it was necessary to put a lot of feed in the swim quickly. In the centre is a brass baitdropper, used for placing your proposed hook-baits hard on the bottom. On the top is the conventional block-end feeder with a permamently stapled base cap and a removable lid for loading. All are part of the barbel fisherman's armoury.

feeder which, not surprisingly, is blocked both ends. One end is permanently blocked and the other has a removable cap enabling you to fill it up with loose feed. When fishing hemp and caster as loose feed it is a good idea to drill the holes a bit larger so that the current washes the grains out more quickly. In deep, heavy currents like the River Severn you are going to need additional weight to make the feeder hold its position. These weights are called ski leads and can be attached, or detached, very easily. In boulder-strewn swims you may need to get the feeder up off the bottom quickly, either to clear the snags or keep a fish off the bottom. There are now planing feeders that whip up off the bottom when retrieved. If you groundbait heavily you can squeeze a ball of groundbait around a wire cage, thus keeping the feed and hook-bait in close proximity.

Additional Equipment

Ledger weights are now all sold in toxic-free compounds. They are expensive so look after them carefully and don't drop them in the grass. I suggest a weight called the Arseley bomb which is pear shaped with a barrel-shaped swivel set into the top. But take a few flat leads with fitted swivels as well as they come in handy when fishing fast, shallow runs where bomb leads are easily dislodged.

Other tackle items you will need are a pair of long-nosed forceps, a weighing sling and scales, and adjustable rod rests. Landing nets should be bought with barbel in mind as you will inevitably hit both species in one session sooner or later. As for keepnets, go for the largest knotless variety you can find not because you want to fill it up but in order to give the fish as much room as possible. Barbel, in particular, do not fare well in a keepnet. If a barbel is really exhausted after a long fight, by all means rest it for a while in a keepnet but be warned that the dorsal fin, once split at the front edge, leaves a serrated bone which can catch in the mesh, trapping the fish and possibly drowning it. Carefully pegging out the net and placing the barbel in head upstream can help to alleviate this but in all honesty the barbel is far better being released straight away. Chub keep well

Tackle Suggestions

In you come my beauty! The author hoops round the rod to its maximum, lifting the barbel's head so that it slides over the rim of the net. Note that he is standing downstream from the fish so that it has to fight both the current and the bend of the rod.

but you often get a few loose scales. Always shorten the catch up to the top two rings of the keepnet while the net is in the water before you lift them from the water. On no account lift the net out with all the chub compressed into the bottom ring and then upend the net to shoot them all down the tube to crash on the ground. Believe me, I still see this done, even with match anglers.

When photographing a barbel do so as quickly as possible. This species suffers greatly in the hands of the inexperienced holiday angler who in a day or week's fishing may only catch a couple of fish. I appreciate that the angler often wants a record of his or her achievements but why leave the fish out on the bank while you rummage through the tackle box to find weighing bag, scales and camera? Put the fish back in the landing net after unhooking it to give it a breather, put your foot on the pole and then sort out all the gear. At least the fish will be fresher and have a better chance of survival. The barbel is basically a river species, but they don't appear in every river and stream in England. Look after them, otherwise the day will come when there are none left for us to catch at all.

Baits

Both chub and barbel will take the same baits, but the chub is more likely to take anything it can safely fit inside its capacious mouth.

Maggots

The best bait for both species, and the one most used by anglers is the maggot. I personally sing the praises of regular white maggots, with the emphasis on quantity but other anglers swear by red maggots. For barbel I feel the colour of the maggot is unimportant; it's the quantity put in that turns them on. For chub, especially in heavily fished venues, feeding red maggots or bronze maggots during the cold winter months does seem to be more productive. I suggest this may be due to the fact that most matchmen follow this practice and so if everybody is using either red or bronze maggots the quantity factor comes into force again. I like to keep my maggots in bran not so much to scour them, as bran is supposed to do, but to remove the smell of ammonia they give off when feeding. I often sprinkle some flavouring into the bait box just to offset this smell.

Go Fishing for Chub and Barbel

If you hook a good barbel, don't be afraid to call on the services of another angler to help with the netting. It's better to get the fish in quickly and then return it as soon as possible rather than playing it for too long and letting it gas up.

Casters

These are probably the best bait for chub in winter. If you can afford to keep up a constant flow of casters the chub will almost go mad to pop the caster and get the juice inside but of course you still have to hook them. Feeding to such a degree will preoccupy the fish and you must use a single caster at a time. While maggots can produce any size of fish, the caster has always been renowned for drawing a better quality fish, especially with chub. On match stretches where barbel are found, barbel also feed on the matchmen's caster, but not so well on the float as they do on the feeder. Casters are an expensive form of bait but certainly worth using during the winter months.

70

Baits

Luncheon Meat

This either comes in a tin, which means you can keep it as long as you want until opened and then it lasts only a day in summer, or you can buy it fresh in a block from the delicatessen counter. Although I keep a few tins for backup, I much prefer the fresh version which has a higher meat content. Many anglers, however, feel the more fat the better, so if you're one of them, why not try this method? Melt some fat in a frying pan and cut up your luncheon meat into the cubes you want to use. Drop them into the hot fat for a few seconds, roll them out onto a plate and let them cool. You can't get much more fat than that! As to size, well for barbel, the bigger the better but having said that a tiny piece on a size 12 hook works well at the back of a swimfeeder full of maggots. If the stretch you are fishing receives a lot of attention from other anglers after barbel, instead of cutting the meat into cubes, take a sharp penknife and trim them into round balls. A finicky barbel will often take a different shape and before you know it you'll be on full alert. I have, of course, taken chub on meat but I don't regard it as particularly successful for big chub. Don't forget you can now get luncheon meat extract flavourings from your local tackle shop, so why not try dipping your maggots into a bottle before you cast out?

Cheese

This has to be my favourite chub bait. Good old Edam used to be my favourite but it has been superseded by plain English Cheddar. It really doesn't matter what cheese you use as long as you can get it to stay on the hook. Years ago there used to be a soft cheese made by kneading cheese into fibres of cotton wool. This may still be worth a try but if you stick to the mild cheeses you will find they don't crumble so much—just a couple of squeezes and you can mould them around the hook. Barbel take cheese readily too which is why I love to use it on a venue where both species occur and it also eliminates the attentions of lesser species like roach and dace. In summer keep your cheese cool in an ASW coolfishbag with a blue freezer block. If you do not use all the cheese in one go, take it home and keep it in the freezer until next time. I generally use between 1 lb and $1^1/4$ lb during a session.

Worms

Worms may be an old fashioned form of bait but they are excellent for winter chub and barbel. No need to worry about redworms or tiger-stripe brandlings, just get hold of the biggest lobworm you can find, impale it a couple of times and send it out. Allow the bite twitches to develop as this is a big bait and both chub and barbel require a couple of seconds to get it all inside their mouths. Worms are a good standby bait when all else fails, particularly in the winter

When using worms as a bait, put two or three on the hook at once. Both chub and barbel will take large baits.

Baits

when cheese can go hard in the cold water and reduce hooking properties. Forget about the 'tail of the lob' theory, put the whole lot out and wait for the fish to find it. A final tip is to break a piece of tail off with your thumb nail before you cast out in order to let those seductive body juices trickle out.

Hemp

This is not much good as a hookbait but when cooked properly until it turns black and the shell splits, this species can drive both species out of their weedbeds. It is best fished as a loose feed in conjunction with caster, the latter being used as a hook-bait. Some venues have banned it as a result of its success and there has been speculation that it is a drug that affects the fish which I find ludicrous. When the seed is cooked the germ is killed so it cannot grow anyway. Try using crushed hemp as a groundbait additive.

Meats

I once saw an 11-lb barbel caught on a piece of fat from a sandwich, so I wouldn't be at all surprised if this species sampled almost any meat baits. Certainly cooked, cold sausage was all the rage 20 years ago and it still works today. Having had some success with most sausage varieties I have to tell you about a real cracker for catching barbel that was 'discovered' by a friend from Essex, Jerry Airey. Try using 1-in. lengths of Ye Old Oak Hot Dog sausages. You may need a piece of twig or a stem of grass in the bend of the hook to stop it falling off as the meat is very soft but it's deadly and Jerry and I have been getting fish on it for a while now while others around us draw blanks. I don't know if it's the distinctive hot dog smell or the fact that the meat is soft but I certainly know it catches fish. I also think barbecue flavour would be successful for barbel, but I have yet to try it myself. As yet I have not managed to catch chub on these hot dog sausages which implies they are an acquired taste.

Go Fishing for Chub and Barbel

Bread

I have taken barbel on breadflake but I feel it should only be used as a winter bait, particularly during periods of heavy frost, or after snowmelt has entered the river and you need a soft bait to pull the hook through on the strike. It is far more successful when used at the end of the season when the weed has died back after heavy frosts and the floods have drained away. Use several loaves mashed up with some groundbait and fish flake under the float, long trotting for chub. This is called 'stodging' in Hampshire and Dorset. Large pieces of flake on anything up to a size 4 hook can be used and as well as catching chub, you are likely to take river roach using the same method.

Chips

I used to use these many moons ago. They are not the best bait for barbel but chub love them, either freelined or floatfished during dusk, when every other bait has failed. The best chips to use are the big fatty variety from the local chippy—without the salt and vinegar!

Slugs

A useful, 'natural' bait for chub. There is no need to split them open as the old books advised, just hook them through once and ledger them in a known chub swim. They are most successful in summer when the chub are still near the beds of streamer weeds.

Crayfish

A good bait for chub, especially the larger chub of slower rivers. Crayfish are difficult to get hold of today, as they are very susceptible

Baits

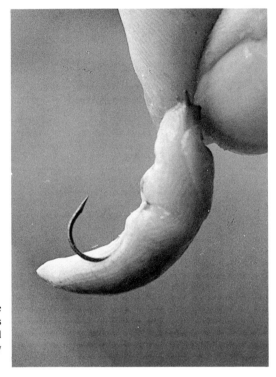

An old-fashioned bait, but one that still works, is the slug. Slugs can be obtained easily and ledgered on the bottom they often produce large specimens.

to pollution and only live in clean rivers. Wait a couple of seconds for the bite to develop when ledgering as the crayfish will tweak the quivertip by itself. Smaller crayfish are the best bet. Keep them alive in an aerated bucket of fresh water, not tap water.

Paste Baits

The best and certainly the quickest to mix up is trout pellet paste. Scald some trout pellets for 30 seconds, strain immediately then allow them to cool until you can squeeze them into a paste. If you want to keep the paste soft just add a little water and squeeze it through again. Quite a messy job but worth it. You can also freeze this bait and thaw it out in about 10 minutes at 'defrost' in a microwave oven.

Go Fishing for Chub and Barbel

This enables you to wait until the last possible moment if you are unsure about weather and river conditions. I have had limited success with using it in conjunction with a float for chub but have fared better with barbel especially on a ledger. Night fishing for barbel is where it really scores.

Boilies

These ready-made carp baits are making an impact on the river scene. Specialist anglers feeding mini-sized boilies into a swim and then fishing standard-sized boilies over the top have been doing well with barbel. Personally I have not been very successful when fishing boilies under the float and find they do better on a static ledger rig. Try bolt-rig techniques for yourself however and come to your own conclusions.

Wasp Grubs

Wasp grubs really come into the fringe category of good baits. They certainly catch chub but they are not the easiest baits to get hold of.

A wasp 'cake' with the grubs extracted. A great bait for the chub fisherman but difficult to get at when the wasps are still present.

Baits

Contact your local council pest control department and ask if you can go along when they have two or three wasp nests to remove. That way they get all the stings and you get all the wasp grubs! Use a fine wire hook as the grubs are very soft. Attach a single wasp grub on the hook and loose feed with gozzer maggots which are the largest sort you can get. Wasp grubs are essentially floatfishing baits and although good for chub they are poor for barbel. I believe dace and roach may tear the grub's skin before the barbel gets a chance to find them and once split, the small fish will eat the body contents.

Sweetcorn

This is the only 'seed' bait I am going to mention due to the fact that there has been much harm done to carp and tench stocks by not cooking the baits properly. All nut and seed baits catch fish but I must stress the importance of boiling them until either the skin of the seed splits, or the nut is soft. Sweetcorn comes either frozen in packets or ready cooked in tins and is harmless. You can squeeze one of the kernels between your thumb and forefinger and find it bursts easily. There's no need to cook it, just defrost it if necessary and use straight away. I confess to not having taken big bags of chub on sweetcorn but provided you can put enough in, the barbel go well on it. One of the best methods is to thread several grains up the hook shank and over the eye making what we in the barbel world call a 'necklace'. This eliminates bites from small fish yet seems perfectly acceptable to the barbel. If you have to scale down to either a single or double grain on a large hook, make sure the hook is a gilt pattern, disguising it against the gold of the sweetcorn. This bait sinks quite fast if you decide to loose feed it but lies well on a bed of groundbait when put in with a baitdropper.

All of the baits mentioned above will catch chub and barbel but if you would like more details I suggest you turn to one of my other books, also published by Oxford Illustrated Press *The Graeme Pullen Guide to Freshwater Fishing Baits*.

Barbel

As an all-round fishing writer I am frequently asked to name the species I favour most. This is almost impossible when you consider the whole range of different freshwater and saltwater fish, each with their own particular qualities. Some species don't fight gamely but I may still find them exciting to pursue. A 400-lb marlin on 50-lb class tackle can fight extremely well but then so can a 6-lb bonefish on 4-lb line in only 6 inches of water! Nevertheless, of all the freshwater species, the barbel, closely followed by the pike, takes the top spot.

I have taken barbel by ledgering a swimfeeder, not by preference but because the situation has demanded it. I have also landed good barbel to over 9 lb on $2^1/2$-lb match tackle but I can't say I really enjoyed it. I was well aware of what I had hooked, but on such light tackle I was unable to control the fight at all. You certainly can land such fish on light tackle but there is no particular skill in it—it often just means you are prepared to wait longer for the fish to tire than many anglers. A long fight with a barbel also does the fish no good at all. I like to fight the fish harder, get it in, then get it back in the water as soon as possible.

My favourite method for taking barbel is to long trot with a piece of luncheon meat under the float, especially if I can get in the water with them wearing a pair of Mukluk chest waders to keep out the cold. In the height of summer you can actually get in the gravel runs between the beds of streamer weed and see the barbel take the bait. The British record for barbel over the past 30 years has remained

Barbel

When unhooking barbel use either a plastic disgorger or a pair of forceps. They have a tough, rubbery mouth and the hook will seldom pull free once you have struck. They are a great fighting species so take care of them and get them back in the water quickly.

below 15 lb although I have heard reports of 20-lb fish being caught which seems quite feasible when one considers the increasing number of properly equipped, specialist anglers now fishing for big barbel. The pressure is certainly on for a new British record. In Europe, especially in eastern European countries, barbel are thought to reach over 25 lb in weight.

The barbel is an exceptionally fine-looking fish. Long and streamlined, with a flat stomach for hugging the gravel on those faster stretches of river, it has a bronze and olive-green sheen that even a painter could not reproduce. There are four barbules situated around the extremities of the mouth which presumably the barbel uses for locating food hidden beneath stones. The snout is pointed with tough, rubbery lips which root around on the river bed. The eyes are small and pig-like and the grey-green fins have an orange tinge to them. In clear water the barbel can often be located by its pectoral

Go Fishing for Chub and Barbel

A beautiful gravel run suited to both chub and barbel. The careful introduction of loose feed will bring the species out from under the weed where they can actually be seen to take the hook-bait.

and ventral fins that stand out against the gravel.

The barbel spawn from May to mid-June although after a cold spring I have seen them spawning on shallow gravel runs as late as early July. On these occasions, one larger female is usually surrounded by smaller males. If you put a bait to them they rarely spook, and will in fact feed vigorously just after spawning, the smaller males being the first to get the bait. It is thought that barbel spawn in feeder streams and tributaries and I have certainly seen them in shallower stretches of the main river. The eggs or roe are said to be poisonous.

The barbel's diet consists of insects, shrimps, other coarse fish eggs, snails and even it seems, small fish. Two 14-lb barbel were taken by salmon anglers during the coarse fishing close season and other anglers have caught barbel while freelining minnows for trout and chub. Presumably other small coarse fish species either spawn on the same gravel area as the barbel or the barbel actually move on to the

A great fight and the fish is in the net. This Hampshire Avon barbel fell to luncheon meat rolled around the tail of the weirpool, the author feeling for bites by touch-ledgering.

Above: An angler floatfishing for barbel on the River Kennet in Berkshire. Sometimes a moving bait can be more successful than a static one.

Facing page: The Water Authority weedcutter spells doom to many of the barbel specialists' favourite swims. This bailiff at the Throop Fishery on the Dorset Stour is doing the job correctly, getting in and manually cutting strips in the weed in order to clear excessive growth and create fishable swims for anglers.

Above: Hemp, caster and a swimfeeder—all you need to get the barbel interested.

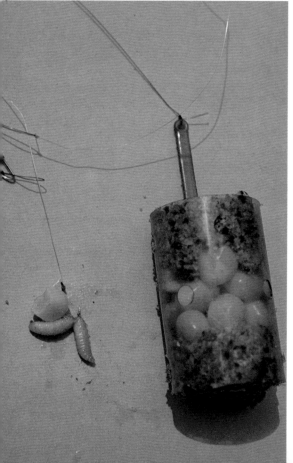

Left: Tipping off a sweetcorn bait with a couple of maggots makes a good 'cocktail' and the movement of the maggots will be an additional attraction.

Above: The author looks pleased with this chunky five pounder taken on cheese intended for chub. Even a 2-lb barbel will give a hard fight.

Below: The author's most successful barbel bait to date—hot dog segments. They require a tiny support in the bend of the hook to prevent them casting off; try a grass stem or tiny twig.

The Gudgeon (above) is often mistaken for a baby barbel (below) but in fact the latter is rarely caught by anglers, even when small baits are being used.

Evening draws in and a barbel angler waits for that magic hour when his rod might leave the rest. Barbel are known for feeding hard in the failing light but they don't continue all through the night.

Essex angler Jerry Airey looks happy with his largest ever barbel taken at Throop Fishery on the Dorset Stour.

gravel beds to feed on fry shoals. Certainly a dead minnow rolled around a weir pool very early in the season has every chance of being taken by a barbel, although I wouldn't be surprised if it went to a big perch or chub instead.

The barbel is only found in a limited number of our rivers and if you do take one you should fully appreciate its tremendous fighting qualities. I have caught hundreds of barbel and so far I have never had one that was a poor scrapper. Quite why they fight so hard I don't know but it may be something to do with the conditions of their environment. The river current makes them work just to stay in position, helped no doubt by their flat belly which allows them to stay near the area of minimal flow. Water pressure on the barbel's curved forehead also presses the fish down onto its belly—another force to be reckoned with. Even its feeding pattern requires considerable effort; rooting around in gravel beds and turning over stones. The barbel has learnt to be persistent and isn't likely to give in easily.

Care should be taken when playing this fish. I personally like to play my fish, regardless of the species, as hard as the tackle will allow but it is a well known fact that the more you put pressure on a barbel the harder the fish pulls back. You can actually get barbel coming towards you with just a nice steady bend in the rod without resorting to any violent pumping and winding. There is, of course, a very fine line between allowing a fish to come gently and pussyfooting around with a good fish for an extensive period of time. The barbel will fight for as long as its strength holds out and I have seen dozens of anglers just keep a tiny bend in the rod and let the fish career about all over the river. I have never said anything because if I told them to put more pressure on and the hook-hold gave out I would be highly unpopular. Nevertheless, if a barbel is played for long periods, especially in hot, low-water conditions during the summer, it can actually die from exhaustion. The best thing to do is to get the fish in with as much even pressure as the tackle will allow rather than dragging the fight out for 15 minutes or more.

Something else to look out for is the barbel suffering from a build up of gases. An angler may net a fish, unhook it, weigh it, photograph it and drop it back in the water. At first glance, the fish

Go Fishing for Chub and Barbel

Proof that the matchman's tactics work. Ringwood member Ray Wales took this fine specimen on a single maggot ledgered upstream of the Ringwood town stretch on the Hampshire Avon.

This is the sorry sight if you don't get a barbel back into the water quickly. The death of this 6 or 7-lb fish on the lower Hampshire Avon is a loss to other anglers and puts needless pressure on the future of the species. Treat barbel with care and return them to the water in your landing net while you set up weighing scales and a camera.

looks quite fit and swims away but unseen by the angler, it turns belly up. Alternatively, the fish may suddenly turn belly side up just out of its depth and out of netting range. The gases in the body build up during the fight, almost forming an air bubble in the stomach. It would be like trying to snorkel underwater while having a fully inflated beach ball tied to your foot! What you need to do is hold the fish firmly with its head into the current, until you can either see bubbles pop out or until the fish has fully regained its balance. If you have a fish that doesn't swim away but starts to keel over as soon as you release it, peg it out in a shaded spot until it recovers naturally rather than letting it go and knowing somewhere downstream another angler will fish it out dead. Sometimes bubbles come out by gently stroking the belly from vent to throat, but a much better method is to wade into water at least 3 ft deep and hold the barbel's tail down with its head inclined upwards, still obviously into the current, so that the gases come out.

If you want to get fishing again and you are really worried that the barbel might keel over, gently peg it out in shallow water by placing a pair of rod rests on either side of its body, with the current gently holding the barbel against its pectoral fins. You can open these out and gently push the rests together, leaving the barbel's gills clear, and allowing the fish to regain strength in its own time. This may take between half an hour and an hour but as long as it remains undisturbed, the fish has a much better chance of surviving than if it is left to float belly up and carried downstream in the current to drown slowly. The barbel is a superb fighting fish and demands some respect.

With regard to catching barbel I would personally rule out two of the techniques mentioned previously for chub—fly fishing and surface fishing—but obviously you are free to try them and might have a lucky catch. Fly fishing with a dry fly for a species which is so obviously a river bed feeder does seem a waste of time to me. However, I have night fished for them conventionally, and have even heard tales of them coming up to suck bread lodged on streamer weeds although I cannot see why they should come up to feed. There may indeed be scope for trying a fast sink line in shallow gravel runs where the barbel may chance upon other fry but I would not wish to use this method of wet fly fishing myself and would have no interest in playing a 7-lb barbel on a number 6 fly rod. Surface fishing in any form, with crust, floaters or even partially supported floating baits seems a similarly unsuitable method for a fish living on the bottom but if it appeals to you, give it a try. When fishing more conventional methods, you can use a number of different baits but concentrate on learning the location of the species, and approach with the correct tackle and feed.

Freelining

When freelining you obviously need a heavy bait to get down to the fish as they seldom rise more than a foot or so from the bottom. Luncheon meat, sausage meat, sausage cubes and even big lobworms will get down through the current quite well although this is better suited to the method of chub fishing talked of earlier, and quite frankly I think you will need some sort of weight to keep the bait down near the fish. You can use a link ledger, but it is very difficult to cast accurately when you only have about a 6-in. gap in the streamer weed to aim for; it is very likely to catch and not drop through. When you lift up to recast, you either move the weed and alert the fish, or lose your bait trying to jerk it free. I discovered the technique of placing a swan shot near the bait when the maggot era ended and there was a ban on this bait on the Royalty at Christchurch. I had been catching plenty of barbel on luncheon meat, but I noticed that one angler was getting fish from all sorts of nooks and crannies in the weed, areas that I wouldn't even have classed as fishable. I don't know his name but we nicknamed him Country John from Yeovil. Country John could catch fish from almost anywhere. All he did was put a huge square of luncheon meat on a size 2 carp hook, then pinch on a swan shot directly behind the eye of the hook—on the main line not on a link. You would think the barbel would see or feel a swan shot so close to the hook but he believed that by the time the fish had

Right: On hard-fished waters, the matchmen will often hook big barbel on small hooks and light tackle. Although they break off a good deal of their fish, watching match results can often tell you which swims are most prolific.

felt the shot he had already struck! The weight of the swan shot and the bait allowed him to keep a very tight contact through the line, enabling him to feel the slightest pluck on the bait. It also gave him a well-balanced weight to swing out and drop right into the smallest clearances in the weeds, the ones he knew none of the rest of us ever fished. I still have qualms about using this method but have caught enough fish on it now to know it works. I know freelining usually means using no weight or encumbrance at all on the line but I feel Country John's technique can be classed as freelining as the bait is constantly on the move and the angler remains in close contact with it.

Floatfishing

Floatfishing for barbel is highly successful and is my favourite way of taking them. There are basically two approaches for catching barbel with a float: you can either go to the fish or get the fish to come to you. Much depends on how intensively the water is fished, how many fish there are in that particular stretch and whether the river has some easily recognisable features for holding barbel. Attending matches and noticing the results is often a useful way of telling which swim in a particular stretch of river is producing the fish. This cuts down the time spent searching a stretch and as match anglers only fish for a few hours, there's a good chance that the swim will be vacant for the next day or two. Your approach should be directly linked to the size of your bait. If you are going to try to catch one or two fish then you need a big bait like meat or cheese. If you are hoping to set up stall and draw the fish to you, then you need a lot of tiny baits like seeds, maggots, casters and groundbaits.

Let us take a look at the first method. I class this as long trotting although in fact you can still floatfish a bait at long range. I use the traditional term because you can work the float with a big bait down through the various runs of the streamer weed and search out the barbel without having to stand up and fish on top of a swim. Once you have had a bite or taken a fish from a likely looking area you can move closer, eliminate much of the trotting distance and concentrate on running the float through the water where the fish are most likely to be. For long trotting you can use either a 10 or 11-ft Avon rod. The Ryobi, with a standard top, is fine and I also like to use an old Bruce and Walker Avon rod.

The traditional reel consists of a centrepin which allows line to be drawn off by the pace of the current. While they are pleasant to use and good for putting a lot of pressure on a fish, they are certainly not a necessity. For regular fishing you will probably have a modern fixed spool and this can easily be adapted by leaving the bale arm open and feathering the line out over the spool lip using your index finger. Find a stretch of river that looks as though it should have some fish in it, slide on an Avon float taking at least a swan shot or several AAA, rig it to cock properly, then add a small number 4 shot and keep it down until only a portion of the painted tip is showing. This may seem strange but when you hold back the pace of the float against the flow it will automatically make the float rise higher in the water. Any shot you put on the line should be placed about a foot from the bait. Don't use anything less than 4 lb as your main line—there's no need for a weaker link on the hook.

Plumbing the depth in a river is difficult so take a depth reading as soon as the lead hits the bottom, then bait up with a big bait and cast out. The float will sink almost immediately with the added weight of the bait but raise the rod top ensuring that the float travels more slowly than the current and leaves a 'V'-shape on the surface. The float is in the neck of the 'V', and you should concentrate on it fully. If the bait catches on weed or a stone it will drag the float under sharply. If it's a barbel, the float should disappear in a flash. You soon learn to distinguish between the two. If the bait does hit the bottom and pull the float under either reduce the depth, a few inches at a time, until it only touches once or twice or simply pull the float back against the current so that the bait comes free. The reason for holding the float back against the flow is that water on the surface of a river travels faster than water close to the gravel. Consequently, the float and line would run before the bait, possibly alerting the fish. By holding the float back quite hard, the bait precedes both line and float.

Go Fishing for Chub and Barbel

By using this method of long trotting you can cover up to 25 yds of water at a time, providing the depth is fairly even. If there are any significant changes in the depth you will have to readjust the float setting. Once you discover the area where the barbel are taking, you can add some loose feed using a bait dropper which enables you to get the feed down on the bottom. If the current is fairly steady you can loose feed by hand but personally I like the reassurance of knowing that the baitdropper has at least emptied its contents on the bottom where the barbel are most likely to be. You will notice that I don't put any loose feed in until I have had a bite or taken a fish—there's little point wasting a lot of bait in an area until you've checked whether there are any barbel feeding there. Sometimes, however, I find I'm faced with a long stretch of uniformly deep water, with streamer weeds leaving a long, straight channel. If I am fairly confident, or have been told that the run holds barbel, then I will put in a load of loose feed, worms and luncheon meat before I start

The author fishes at the side of the main sluice of a weirpool and nets a good barbel. Don't neglect the fastest water and remember that the flow on the surface will be faster than the flow near the river bed.

fishing. This will then be taken by fish somewhere along that channel and all I have to do is find out where.

The other method of floatfishing for barbel involves bringing the fish to you by feeding heavily with maggots or casters and hemp. To do this properly the current should be slower, the swim possibly deeper and ideally there should be a large, slack area behind some streamer weed. Start by putting in the maggots or casters with a baitdropper, ensuring you place your dropper in the same place every time—if possible, at the head of the swim. Fish the same Avon float, rod and reel, but drop to 3-lb hook-links, making them about 18 in. long. Other anglers may use shorter ones but from my experience, larger ones are better. The maggots will probably wriggle down in between the stones, so they will not be whisked away as quickly as you think.

Obviously you are going to lose a lot of bait to dace and roach, and you will probably have to take a lot of these before the barbel push them out. Some anglers really heap in the feed in an effort to gorge the small fish completely, leaving the barbel free to move in. Until the barbel locate the stream of maggots, you may need to let the float tackle run some way down the swim before retrieving. Set the float so that the bait trips over the bottom, then hold the float back so that the bait precedes it. Your hook size should be a 16 if you're fishing single and double maggots, or a 14 or 12 if you want to fish a bunch. Sometimes it is worth starting off with 4 or 5 maggots as this avoids the attentions of all but the most enthusiastic dace or roach, and barbel are going to be less choosy when they first feed. As they feed more heavily, and possibly see a mate or two depart to your net, they may get wary and take only double or single maggots on a size 16. I see no point in using smaller hooks—despite the barbel's rubbery lips you might still pull it out.

When the fish really get their heads down into the maggots, it is up to you to keep them there. This means more baitdroppers of loose samples. Rather than putting just a single one down every trot through, I like to put at least six in at one go, thereby disturbing the swim only once every 20 minutes. If you are chalk stream fishing you can see them working up the swim to where the maggots are dropped. You will notice that initially they come up, take a few, then turn into the shade of the streamer weed and swim right down before emerging at the tail end of the swim. When they gain confidence they will stay longer over the baited area and also swim down a shorter distance before swimming back up again. Consequently, make your trots through the swim shorter and shorter as the fish gain confidence. In spate rivers you are not going to be able to see the fish through the water but will find that the bites are starting to come nearer and nearer the baited area. That gives you the cue to start short trots through.

If you can manage to get enough loose feed then I think this is the best way to successfully *hook* barbel on the float. Many of you will be thinking that a 3-lb hook-link is rather light and will perhaps want to go back to 6 or 8 lb straight through. The problem here is that a couple of maggots in the water have virtually no weight and the thicker nylon of, for example, 8 lb will be less flexible, making the maggots go through without any movement at all. By using lighter line the maggots can swing around in any smaller undercurrents, thus appearing as natural as possible to the barbel. If you do hook one on 3-lb line, you should of course try to get below the fish. Unless the swim is very clear, there is no way the barbel will come up through a weedbed against the flow of the current on 3-lb line.

I would, in fact, advise putting the pressure on from below a fish on any line. That way you are making it fight not only the current, but if it gets stuck in a bed of streamer weed you can usually make it kick itself free if you're pulling from a downstream position.

Never point the rod at a fish that is snagged and walk backwards for a break. Always give them the chance to free themselves or at least change position and let some of the weed come free. If necessary, put the rod down in a rest, slacken off the drag and watch the tip for a few minutes. Once it starts to move, wind up the drag and pile on the pressure to keep the fish moving. Another tip worth mentioning applies if you have stopped a fish that is heading towards a weedbed or one that is burying itself in a weedbed. The problem with pumping a fish, especially when using a fixed spool reel, is that you have to drop the rod top to ease the pressure and gain some line. With a centrepin you can actually wind all the time so the problem is not so pronounced. Once you ease the pressure in order to take a few

Barbel

Try to keep the barbel's head facing towards you when you slide the net under it so that any sudden surges will help push the fish into the landing net rather than away from it. The picture shows a River Kennet fish.

turns of the handle, the fish can move off again and once it has started, it is difficult to stop. My advice is that if you have the fish coming and it starts to kick for the sanctuary of the weed again, *don't* drop the pressure to retrieve line. Keep the rod high, watch the arc of the rod bend very closely and, keeping the maximum amount of pressure on, just walk backwards a few steps. When the fish is several feet from the weed you can relax the pressure to gain line, safe in the knowledge that you have gained a little space and knowing that you can repeat the tactic again if necessary. Lines down to 3lb b.s. are ideal for this as you can maintain a constant pressure on the fish.

I once did an experiment with some friends in a hotel swimming pool in Kenya. We had been out chasing tuna, sail and striped marlin all day and as usual, went to the pool as soon as we got in. We had our tackle with us, and I bet (without a wager!) that I could stop anyone in the length of that pool on 50-lb line. I actually stopped Pete Haines, our strongest swimmer, on 30-lb test outfits. I can stop most swimmers on 12-lb test lines but give them a pair of flippers and the balance of power is completely different. The only one I lost was Pete, using flippers, who reached the end of the pool. They all agreed that the worst pressure was the pressure applied evenly, leaving you thrashing away with arms and legs but getting nowhere. The same results can be achieved by 'walking' a fish out of a snag—try it and see how effective it is.

Another method of floatfishing for barbel, popular many years ago and still effective today, involves using centrepins. Instead of baiting a run or channel between weedbeds, pile in the loose feed right on top of the tail end of the weedbeds, allowing the bait, usually plain white maggots, to wriggle their way through the weed and sink to the bottom. (This also drives chub completely scatty, and is a very useful method to use on them.) Once the maggots start to hit the bottom, usually slightly down from the tail end of the weed, the barbel will surge around, often making the weed 'hump' as they dive into a feeding frenzy. Once they emerge from under the weed they feel less safe, still taking the maggots but a bit more carefully. Set the float to about 2 ft in depth, cast across the tail of the current and ease the float into position at the tail of the weedbed where the current is less strong. You then slowly pull up the float until it is resting right against the weeds and set the rod in a rest, with the rod pointing straight at the float.

An Alcock's Aerial was the favoured centrepin used with this method. It had a screw that could be tightened to impart pressure on the centre spindle, thereby adding some drag. With the check put on, you could sit comfortably next to the rod, waiting for the float to dive under. If you missed seeing the float go, the ratchet on the centrepin would sound and you grabbed your rod, and lifted into the fish. It would be hard to find a more pleasurable method of taking barbel on a summer's day. First, of course, you need to find a swim that allows you that bit of slack and holds barbel—but then that's always half the problem!

Ledgering

The most productive method of fishing for barbel must however, be

Barbel

ledgering. Barbel feed on the bottom and are bound to congregate where the food is most plentiful so if you put down a bed of bait, closely followed by your hook-bait, you should be on to a winner. In the Victorian and Edwardian eras, anglers took nearly all their fish by ledgering. They knew the importance of good groundbaiting and would even pre-bait a swim several days prior to fishing it with chopped up worms mixed into 'clay balls', a gunk of mud and worms compressed into a ball and thrown out. Greaves, a by-product of tallow candle making, was also a common groundbait and I can only assume the mixture gave off some sort of fatty substance. Now we have the opportunity to use all sorts of cereal based groundbaits, together with additives, colourings and flavourings. Whether any of the current flavourings actually attract fish or whether they just remove any human scent I am still unclear. Years ago it was certainly thought necessary to remove any smell of tobacco although today this is a much less common problem.

Groundbaiting

Whatever groundbait you choose, it is important to make up a firm mix to ensure that it holds for some time in fast water, only breaking up gradually. You should therefore avoid any fine cloudbaits, bran based mixes or brown crumb mixes. Indeed you will probably find it difficult to get it to the river bed anyway without it crumbling in the current. The best groundbait I have found and used for years is a coarse white crumb, mixed about eight to one with some golden breadcrumb. On its own golden breadcrumb produces too stiff a groundbait. There are three different ways to bait up properly and all can be used in a barbel swim of your choice. They will work in a slack area behind a weedbed or out in a channel of faster flowing water between some streamer weed. You can either use the groundbait 'straight', and then use a baitdropper to position your loose feed of hook samples on top of the carpet of groundbait balls; or you can mix the hook samples in as you make up the groundbait (casters, crushed hemp, maggots, etc), or you can 'cup' the groundbait balls and fit the maggots inside the ball.

The first method is easy, you just mix up the groundbait, taking care not to make it too sloppy. If it is too dry and will not bind, add more water sparingly until you can squeeze it into a firm ball. Before you throw it in, dip your groundbait ball into the water by hand—less will then break off the outside of the ball when it hits the water. Mix up several balls, ensuring they are the same size, then aiming for the desired spot, fire the balls out in quick succession, making a mental note of where they hit. Then put in as much loose feed as you can afford, casting to exactly the same spot with the baitdropper. When you cast out, remember to allow for the fact that the swimfeeder might swing a bit further down in the current and any groundbait that breaks up with the action of the current will trail downstream.

The second method is virtually the same except you mix in your required hookbait to the groundbait mix, squeeze the lot together as described above and throw it in the swim. This is the simplest method and probably the best way for beginners to start.

Finally there is the 'cup' technique in which you mix up the groundbait as before then hollow out each ball and fill it with maggots. Take another handful of wet groundbait and squeeze it over the top to form a lid. Dip it under water for a second and then throw it, as quickly as possible, out into the swim. If the water is clear and the balls lie closely grouped together that's fine but if they move off downstream before breaking up you need some additional weight. This is achieved by pushing a stone into the base of the hollowed out ball before you put in the maggots. You will be surprised at the difference this makes. The wriggling action of the maggots inside the ball will break it up and they will spill out into a very confined area, whereas a mix with feed in it will release the feed too quickly under fast current conditions. Years ago this was a standard method on the lower Hampshire Avon and when the barbel really got their heads down, they would swim right up and pick up a whole groundbait ball, shaking it to break it open and get at the maggots inside. Even now I still see this happen, although I must be one of the few who take the trouble to 'cup' their groundbait balls with maggots.

Left: A nice haul of River Kennet barbel. Barbel do not fare well in keepnets and should only be held long enough for them to recover. The dorsal fin can often snag in the net so try to return the fish as soon as possible after unhooking it.

Go Fishing for Chub and Barbel

Swimfeeders

Once you have completed the groundbaiting, you need to know what ledger rig to use. We have already discussed fishing with a standard ledger in the section about bigger baits and for fishing over concentrated groundbait the swimfeeder is undoubtedly the best method although I do not particularly like using one. When you are fishing either of the three mentioned groundbait techniques then use the open-ended feeder. You may have to drill out the holes of the feeder a bit more to let the feed come out. I like to use my feeders on about 10 in. of link, as a running ledger rig. Squeeze some groundbait into one end of the feeder to provide a cap of sorts, put in your maggots, caster, hemp or whatever, then plug up the other end with groundbait. If you put in too much groundbait you will squash the maggots and the feeder does not empty properly. Too little and the 'plug' flies out as soon as it hits the water and all the contents drift away on the current, right over the heads of the barbel. The chub, roach and dace will appreciate this, as they will chase downriver and get a free feed but the barbel remain unimpressed!

When feeding hard you occasionally get staggering bites that threaten to pull the rod into the water. If the crash-take is fairly even in movement it implies that a barbel has picked up the entire plastic feeder and is shaking it about to release the contents inside. If the bite jams down quickly but then springs up straight, it's a good bet that you've got a 'liner', a barbel that was rooting around over the feed when it crashed into your line. That means you are casting out a bit too far; the feeder is outside the baited patch but the main line is lying across it. Drop your next cast in a few feet shorter and the next fish should stay attached. You can use a quivertip if you have one but quite honestly, once the barbel get their heads down, you are going to see the bite well enough.

Much has been written about the power of a barbel bite but I assure you this is not always the case. On heavily fished waters where the feeder is standard practice, those same fish will gently ease up to the feeder and just lie directly behind it, gently picking off the maggots or casters as they drift downstrean. Barbel are also quite capable of picking up a bunch of maggots, feeling the nylon

104

Barbel

Snow has cloaked the countryside in a white blanket but the chub angler will still find that his species are in a feeding mood. While the barbel tend to get lethargic in very cold weather, the chub feed heartily.

hook-link, and spitting them out without imparting more than a tremble to the rod top. To the inexperienced angler they could just be dace or roach tweaking at the maggots but if in doubt, strike! It's certainly worth putting up a rod with a quivertip if the fish are difficult.

The length from the feeder to the hook is also quite an important factor. You can vary it to suit yourself but as a rule, if the fish are feeding well I would advise a short link of maybe 6 in. but if the fish are hard, as a result of the water being match-fished by feeders, then I would set the hook about 15–18 in. from the feeder. With a long hook length you definitely need a quivertip to pick up the indistinct bites but if the hook-link and feeder are closer together, an ordinary ledger rod will do.

The barbules around the fish's mouth must make it more conscious than some species of everything just outside the fringe of its lips.

Go Fishing for Chub and Barbel

Barbel seem to root around for food, then move off quite quickly downstream before returning up the swim again. When a barbel picks up maggots or casters it may not feel the 3 or 4-lb line so it moves off downstream and then suddenly feels the drag of the line. As it is already moving downstream, it merely has to kick its tail into third gear which, aided by the flow of the river, undoubtedly accounts for some of those incredible rod-buckling bites.

One of the older types of feeder that capitalised on this habit of the barbel was the original block-end feeder. This had a fixed plastic cap on one end and a removable plastic cap on the other. The feeder was filled with maggots, no groundbait, the cap replaced and it was fished as usual. It was a very handy feeder and should be used even now when you fish using groundbait balls with maggots cupped inside them. The barbel soon grabs the groundbait balls and shakes them in a frenzy to get at the maggots. Once a ball splits open, a cloud of white maggots bursts out and several barbel immediately rush in to mop them up. With the older block-end feeder the main line ran right through the middle of the feeder cap lids and the feeder was held about 6 in. from the hook. On the other end of the feeder, above it on the main line, was another shot, tightly pinched on about 6 in. up. Therefore, when a barbel picked up a bait and moved more than 6 in. downstream, it would come up against the second stop shot, panic, and then bolt downstream, virtually hooking itself in the process. Of course some barbel did still occasionally free themselves but often, the weight of the feeder alone, dragging behind the fish, held a small, sharp hook in place until the angler could reach for a rod.

This procedure was standard practice for match fishing and was used a lot by London anglers on the Thames and Hampshire Avon to good effect. It was affectionately known as the 'hanger', due to its self-hooking ability. Initially some matches banned the use of the swimfeeder as being unfair to float fishermen but it is still used and remains one of the best ways to take a barbel. It might be worth noting that 'back-stopping', or putting the shot above the feeder, is a technique used a lot by carp anglers who use bolt-rigs to catch their fish. There was recently some controversy about back-stopping, as a fish that is broken off drags the lead around until it snags on something and then dies. Many carp were discovered dead in a

Barbel

An angler reaches the final stages of a battle with a Kennet barbel. When fishing from a high bank, take an extendible landing net pole to reach down to the fish. Make sure most of the keepnet is in the water.

Go Fishing for Chub and Barbel

Hampshire Club water as a result of being broken off on back-stop rigs. Back-stopping has now been banned on this and other waters. Personally, I don't like to see a barbel dragging a feeder around until it snags up and drowns and I wonder if back-stopping should not be banned completely—after all, there is enough pressure on fish today without adding to the problem.

I often use a similar method of hooking finicky barbel that does not involve back-stopping or run the risk of a snagged fish if you break off. All you need to do is overweight your feeder by adding a ski lead, even though the current doesn't demand it. You want to be able to tighten down on the feeder as much as possible but without adding so much pressure that you pull it out of position, hence the need for over weighting. My feeder is on a running ledger rig, held simply by two plastic ledger stops positioned next to each other, avoiding any slippage during the cast. If I do have the misfortune to break a fish off, the line slips through the swivel, leaving the feeder to free fall. Fishing recently on the Dorset Stour, I took a fish on a feeder and it ran me straight through a bed of spearweed in the centre of the river. There was no way out and eventually the line parted. Later that evening I hit a fish on a ledgered hot dog cube and was amazed to find my own hook and a double ledger stop on its lip but no feeder. It had slipped free obviously causing the fish no distress otherwise it would not have taken the bait again.

When you cast out your over-weighted feeder, let it settle, then position your rod rests so that the rod points straight at the feeder. There should be no bend in the tip, in fact all you need is a good ledger rod, not even a quivertip. Wind up tight until you feel the feeder bump once, then jam a piece of foam into the first butt ring and take the anti-reverse off the reel. The foam stops water pressure from rotating the reel handle and causing the line to bag out. This creates the same effect as back-stopping in as much as any barbel moving away will come up against the reel and wind back the handle as it bolts away. Just make sure you sit next to the rod!

An alternative is to leave the reel in gear, with the anti-reverse on but slacken off the reel drag. On slow sessions for big fish I find this a better method as you can look around and still hear the drag squeal as the fish takes. When using small baits such as mini boilies, maggots or casters, the fish hook themselves better due to the smaller hook size. Whatever hook you use, make sure that the wire is very strong and not prone to straightening. On a hard fished match water it may be the single maggot that the biggest fish in that stretch takes, and you need to take it just a little carefully near the net where the cushioning effect of the line is at a minimum.

Stret-Pegging

There are a couple of other methods of ledgering that I use myself both for entertainment value and for winkling out the odd single fish. One of these is stret-pegging, a method of floatfishing used for combating a downstream wind that tends to drag normal floats too fast. A slight upstream breeze is ideal as it bellies out the line above

The River Kennet in Berkshire. One of the more popular venues for small to medium-sized barbel.

the float a little and helps you to hold back when trotting through. It almost falls within the category of ledgering, as it is done with the depth set deeper than it should be, up to a quarter of the actual depth of the swim. Cast out and let the tackle bump around by holding the float back hard, letting it come to rest just below you. The bait should be static for as long as seems necessary. To move it further down the swim you simply lift the rod top, the shot comes off the bottom, the bait drifts down and you lower the rod top again. Let it rest there for a while, open the bale arm, let a yard or so of line spill out, close the bale arm, then lift the rod to dislodge the shot again. Stret-pegging used to be a common means of searching a swim and keeping a bait in different areas without continually casting and perhaps disturbing the barbel.

Trundling

A variation on stret-pegging is something I call 'trundling' which comes in useful when I want a bait, usually a large piece of luncheon meat, to trip on the bottom at the same pace as the current but through very narrow channels in between weedbeds. Again this involves oversetting the depth of the float but not to the same extent as when stret-pegging. I find about one foot over about right. I then bunch the shot together about 6–8 in. from the hook. Freelining or light link-ledgering such narrow channels can be a problem and often my main line catches the nearside edge of the weed and impedes the natural speed of the bait. Every time I try to lift the rod top the bait catches in the weed and I am unable to run the bait through evenly. This problem is accentuated the further away you are from the channel. Fishing a channel one third or three quarters away across a river means that the angle of the line to the bait is very shallow and the line invariably gets caught in the weed. By using a float set slightly overdepth however, the line from the bait to the rod is straight and I can hold the rod high, thus keeping a tight line from the rod top to the float. All I have to do in order to get the float moving evenly is to raise the rod top and it bumps its way down the swim, rubbing

Barbel

against the nearside edge of the streamer weed. It is also a useful method when casting across river to fish in open water, allowing the bait to work round in an arc. Often you will feel the take through the rod top as the float plunges away. The faster the current the harder the bite.

With the age of modern technology well and truly upon us, there has never been more pressure on all our river and lake species than there is today. Anglers have access to all the latest techniques, the most advanced equipment and a whole range of successful baits. Even the best locations for taking each species are common knowledge. The Dorset Stour, often referred to as the 'Wessex river', is known for holding big barbel. The barbel have been there for years but it is only in the last four or five years that anglers have moved from other rivers to discover the delights of this slow flowing spate river. If a new record emerges, I am fairly confident that it will come from the Dorset Stour. I would even go so far as to say that I think it will just top the 16-lb mark and will come from the stretch of river that flows from Bounds Farm up through West Parley for a few miles. Obviously I cannot specify a particular swim as barbel are known to migrate up and down the river according to the season, particularly in late autumn.

Personally I am not motivated by the thought of breaking a record when fishing for either chub or barbel. For me, the pleasure is derived not just from the pursuit of the quarry but from an appreciation of the environment surrounding the riverside and the world beneath the water's surface. The chub has the appeal of being widely distributed, with an appetite that often makes it obliging to anglers. The barbel is rarer, very powerful and requires a careful approach. You can set up your stall for chub and be lucky enough to hook a barbel or vice versa. The chances are, however, whichever one slides into your net will give you enough satisfaction and excitement to encourage you to learn more about its whereabouts and habits.